Praise for *Does My Voice Matter?*

"There are countless times in our lives when we're faced with the most fundamental questions: Am I important? Do I make a difference? Do I matter? In *Does My Voice Matter?*, Cynthia James offers brilliant guidance and powerful inspiration, as she takes us on a personal journey filled with adventure and transformation. What a wonderful opportunity and resource to help you reinvent your life in a way that reflects how important you truly are."

—MARCI SHIMOFF, #1 *New York Times* bestselling author, *Happy for No Reason* and *Chicken Soup for the Woman's Soul*

"I have loved Cynthia James' voice for decades, but this profound book transforms that love into pure admiration. Cynthia's book helps us to realize that a path to better mental health is understanding that yes, our voices do matter. We all must do everything in our power to listen to other voices, and most importantly, listen to our own. Her moving, important, difficult, and joyous journey inspires us to find that resonant voice within."

—CHARLES RANDOLPH-WRIGHT, award-winning writer, director and producer of television, film and theatre

"Cynthia James is a wonder. Learn from her. Listen to her. Despite growing up on circumstances that would have flattened most of us, she thrived with a natural born grace and spirituality that awes me. She is a living example of the power of prayer, of truth, of goodness. and with this book, she shows us that it is possible, even in these complex and challenging times, to find our own voices."

—GENEEN ROTH, author of m bestsellers including *When Food is Love* ar

T0007288

"I love my colleague and dear friend, Cynthia James! She brings us another landmark book, *Does My Voice Matter?* It is exceptional—in fact, remarkable! With profound vulnerability and insight, she shares defining moments that led her to the embracing and honoring of her authentic voice. Immerse yourself in Cynthia's soul-touching book and share it widely, because we're all here to live our lives ‹out loud› and to shine our Light into this world."

—Dr. Roger Teel, Spiritual Teacher and author
of *This Life is Joy*

"In all her offerings, Cynthia invites the readers to come to their authentic selves, accept the inner guidance offered, and then gives solid, workable tools, to come to a more balanced, peaceful, productive life. Her vehicle this time is her own life's story filled with all its ups, downs, questions, sidetracks, successes, seeming missteps, triumphs and insights. Her honesty about her many different experiences shines a light for all of us seeking a more authentic life."

—Kathleen Noone, Emmy Award winning Actress, Master of
Fine Arts, Master of Spiritual Psychology, Labyrinth Facilitator

"I was spellbound, I couldn't stop reading Cynthia James' book, *Does My Voice Matter?* You feel as though you are right there with her as she shares the extraordinary highs and lows, sorrows, and joys in every part of her amazing life of poverty, stardom, motherhood, womanhood, success and more, showing us that we each have enormous potential and we each are essential."

—Dr. Anita Sanchez, Nahua (Aztec) and Latina, author of
The Four Sacred Gifts: Indigenous Wisdom for Modern Times

"Give yourself the gift of Cynthia James and what you'll receive is the gift of your Self. I felt seen, heard, and empowered from the first chapter. Cynthia's presence on the page and on the stage is like a transmission from a higher realm that leaves you feeling uplifted, inspired, and ready to take on the world. I invite you take this glorious and often humorous adventure of the soul with Cynthia. You'll be the better for it."

—SANDRA JOSEPH, author of *Unmasking What Matters:*
10 Life Lessons from 10 Years on Broadway

"*Does my Voice Matter?* is a deeply passionate tale, a true story how one woman dared to climb her own personal mountain to find her voice and between the lines gives us essential keys to understanding ourselves. Cynthia leaves with us her life lived, as a model for us to climb our own mountain, yell out loud, and listen with joy the sound our own voice."

—SHIRLEY JO FINNEY, award-winning international
director of theater, television and films

Does My Voice Matter?

Does My Voice Matter?

*A JOURNEY OF SELF-DISCOVERY,
AUTHENTICITY, AND EMPOWERMENT*

Cynthia James

SHE WRITES PRESS

Copyright © 2022 Cynthia James

All rights reserved. No part of this publication may be reproduced, distributed, or transmitted in any form or by any means, including photocopying, recording, digital scanning, or other electronic or mechanical methods, without the prior written permission of the publisher, except in the case of brief quotations embodied in critical reviews and certain other noncommercial uses permitted by copyright law. For permission requests, please address She Writes Press.

Published 2022
Printed in the United States of America
Print ISBN: 978-1-64742-243-1
E-ISBN: 978-1-64742-244-8
Library of Congress Control Number: 2022907469

For information, address:
She Writes Press
1569 Solano Ave #546
Berkeley, CA 94707

Interior design by Tabitha Lahr

She Writes Press is a division of SparkPoint Studio, LLC.

All company and/or product names may be trade names, logos, trademarks, and/or registered trademarks and are the property of their respective owners.

Names and identifying characteristics have been changed to protect the privacy of certain individuals.

Contents

Foreword

C ynthia James is the real deal. I should know; I've had the privilege of being her friend for nearly three decades. And I don't mean just a social friend but a true friend. The kind who gets mad at you and picks up the phone to tell it to you straight rather than just cool the connection without giving you the chance to make things right again. The kind you can trust with the truth. The kind to whom you're free to confess your sins, secure in the knowing that you won't be shamed—yet who, you're also acutely aware, will hold you accountable to be who you say you are, and in a way that causes you to grow up and get real. The kind that you can belly laugh with and cry with, dripping snot and all. That kind of friend.

Although I'm now a therapist and teacher with a couple of best-selling books under my belt myself, when I first met Cynthia I was a shy and insecure aspiring singer-songwriter who was doing temp work to pay the rent. I had a burning desire to help others to heal, and a crazy idea about going down to Skid Row to work with women and men who were in a program to recover from homelessness and all that led to it. I wanted to run songwriting workshops and bring in professional songwriters to help tell their stories through song. I had no idea how to accomplish this crazy dream of mine and, frankly, I was in over my head. I'd somehow convinced the Los Angeles Mission to give me a chance, and had scheduled the first creative writing workshop with eighteen women and men from their residential program. Yet having never done this before, I hadn't a clue what to do next, and I was in a panic. That's when someone had the great idea of introducing me to Cynthia.

I remember feeling intimated as she walked into the restaurant. Stunningly beautiful and elegantly dressed, she made me feel self-conscious in my faded black jeans and baggy shirt. Yet the moment she sat down, her smile and warmth melted me. I began to feel like the most important person in the world as I shared my vision with her. In response, she poured out encouragement, kindness, and wisdom. Already a seasoned teacher, Cynthia freely shared her ideas about what I could do with people with such infectious enthusiasm that I became inspired. I got so excited that I actually forgot to be scared. The workshops went on to become a huge success, culminating in a nationally released CD that featured star artists. Yet most rewarding was that it radically transformed the lives of those once homeless men and women who participated.

Cynthia James is modern-day mystic who has direct access to great wisdom and spiritual guidance yet looks nothing like our preconceived notions about mystics—people who are some-how untouched by the temptations and glamour of celebrity, the glitter and decadence of Las Vegas, or the copious affluence and wealth of Hollywood. This girl has pretty much seen and done it all. Yet through the ups and downs and in-betweens, she's always managed to return to the light of love, making truth her home and faith her North Star.

———————————

The wise, sacred, healing messages of hope and inspiration peppered throughout this book are profound. Yet unlike other great spiritual texts, this one's hysterically funny and often had me laughing out loud. At other times, I found myself catching my breath, on the edge of my seat and turning pages as fast as I could, desperate to find out how in the world she'd ever recover from *this*. Her candor about what's it's like to be the only black woman in the room, the humiliating mistakes she's made with the men she's dated, and the rugged uphill road to forgiving the unforgiveable serves as a guide for us all.

It's the stories we share that help us to heal each other's broken hearts, and this book has plenty of them. Not only that, but Cynthia also gives us the opportunity to embark upon our own healing journey by including exercises and practices at the end of every chapter so we can mend right along with her. Yet don't assume this book is just another run-of-the-mill healing workbook. Make no mistake. This book is a page-turner. And it will empower you to live your most magical life, as Cynthia has found her way to hers. For I can say without a shadow of a doubt that Cynthia has one of the most magical lives of anyone I know. Between her delightfully happy marriage to her talented, handsome husband, Carl Studna, her gorgeous and loving home with its restful retreat-center vibe, her brilliant and flourishing creative career, and her beautiful, vibrantly healthy body . . . well, if you want to find out how she manifest this wonderful life (or more importantly, how you can manifest *yours*), put this book by your bedside and make reading it and engaging the practices within it your new daily practice. As you do, you'll discover, once and for all, that the answer to the question posed as the title of this book is a deep and resounding, "Yes!"

—KATHERINE WOODWARD THOMAS, *New York Times*
best-selling author of *Calling in "The One"* and
Conscious Uncoupling

What If?

What if our religion was each other?
If our practice was our life?
If prayer was our words?
What if the temple was the Earth?
If forests were our church?
If holy water—the rivers, lakes, and oceans?
What if meditation was our relationships?
If the teacher was life?
If wisdom was self-knowledge?
If love was the center of our being?

—GANGA WHITE

Introduction

I was born in 1948. That means I have been on this planet for over seventy years. I am amazed as I write this. I don't feel old, but I am clear that I have experienced many things in this lifetime. I have spent years looking for me. Who am I? Why am I here? What is my purpose? Am I important? Does my voice matter? Those questions seemed unsurmountable in my youth, because everything around me was intense.

As a child, I saw possibilities. I saw the goodness in people. Somehow ideas always came to me about how to make things better. In my heart I wanted people to be happy and thrive. That really didn't make sense, because my family life was filled with struggle.

Today, I know the feelings that I had were connected to my spirit, my soul. Something in me knew that there was an interconnectedness in the universe, and I wanted to experience it. That desire, my familial environment, the culture I lived in, and the experiences of humanity made it difficult for me to navigate life. Sometimes I felt at war with myself. As I look back, what I see is how culture, systems, politics, race, and many versions of artistry formed me.

As a coach, teacher, performing artist, and facilitator, I have worked with thousands of people around the world, and there is a common thread. Each person wanted to be authentic, seen, heard, loved, and fully expressed. They all had different stories, but it was clear how cultural and personal experiences had formed them. They also wanted a better world and to be a beneficial presence.

I wondered if my life growth experiences might be a benefit for people looking for their authentic life expression . . . their voice!

I was brought up in a family that had five generations of abuse and trauma. Pain was expected, and dramatic experiences happened consistently. Poor choices in relationships, financial challenges, addictive patterns, and unhealthy habits plagued the entire family. My father was an alcoholic; my stepfather was a wife beater and a pedophile. My mother believed she was powerless. Yet I was different. I was highly expressive and from an early age felt the presence of my inner voice. To show it, I often questioned choices and reactions in my family, church, and community. The feedback was instant and painful. I learned quickly to find ways to protect myself, escape the insanity, and hide the fear, guilt, anxiety, and blame I held deep inside.

It took me a long time to realize that I was not alone. As I began to hear stories that were familiar to my own, I realized that almost everyone I knew was trying to free themselves from their own version of a traumatic or neglectful childhood. Our parents had come out of the war and the Depression and had no tools to manage emotional pain. In my life, domestic violence was the noose around our family's neck. But surprisingly, domestic violence didn't just affect the poor, or people of color, or those struggling with mental illness or addiction. It seemed to be prevalent even in families that appeared to be healthy. I saw young people drinking too much and dabbling in drugs, compulsive shopping, and early sexual experiences. Today I know it was all about numbing out feelings.

People in every walk of life ask, "Does my voice matter?" For me, the question covers a myriad of arenas. It is not just about the sound of the voice. It is about the full expression of the individual. That means it can be spoken, danced, written, painted, and expressed in multiple forms. The important focus is that the voice brings to life the authentic and vulnerable demonstration of each human being.

———————

We live in a critical and oftentimes violent world. People are afraid to talk about what they feel, think, or believe. They withhold energy for fear of being ridiculed, punished, or excluded. Their deepest dreams and desires are hidden away and covered up by doubt, insecurity, old experiences, and fears. People often express the feelings of being imprisoned by their circumstances. In some cases, those feelings are only too real. There has been little support to counteract this message. From religious organizations to governments, educational institutions, and corporations, very little is done to remind people of their inherent beauty, wisdom, grace, and power. In fact, some would say the messages have been the exact opposite. To get ahead, one must conform, follow directions, and not question the rules. For those struggling to find their voice, this recipe is the perfect formula for a life riddled with stagnation, stress, and disengagement.

People that resist the "norm" are often criticized. They are ostracized and made to feel ashamed that they desire to express themselves in ways that make others uncomfortable. Some can resist this kind of negative bombardment for a while, but most eventually fall into line and shut down the parts of themselves that fuel their passion. When this kind of experience happens to people very young in life, their voices are often silenced before they ever have a chance to be heard.

Regardless of when your voice is shut down, the end results are often the same: a deep sense of cynicism, victimization, disconnect, and alienation. The sensation that you do not matter, do not count, and are not here to be heard permeates your very being. And yet the antidote to this experience is to find your voice. To stand up for yourself and demand, in whatever "octave" necessary, that you, too, are important. Then, and only then, will the illusion that you don't count be eradicated from your consciousness.

To escape the dysfunctional reality of my childhood, I discovered ways to bring my voice into the world. I did this through music, dance, and creating a world that was filled with all the possibilities that would allow me to escape my reality and leap into the life I could only find in my dreams. As a child, I was often told to get my head out of the clouds and put my feet on the ground. People took pride in telling me, and this may have come from a good place, that I was poor and it was not going to change.

Introduction

To fight against this dose of reality, I became defiant within myself. Many of my friends were into drugs, inappropriate sexual encounters, and gang experiences. I didn't know how, but I knew this life was not going to become my reality. I made it my business to do the opposite of what I saw.

I excelled in school. I joined the debate and chess teams. I became a cheerleader and secretary of my class. I was selected to be a teen model in a department store, and I sang at school events.

As you might expect, I was often scared to step out, but it felt like it was the only way to free myself from the bondage of my familial beliefs and experiences. My creative essence became my pathway to changing my reality and the doorway to step into a world of awe and wonder—a world where I could be anything I chose to be.

As a child, I had no way of knowing that world events, changemakers, collaborative calls for action, and people willing to challenge the status quo would be catalysts for shaping my views. These things fueled my willingness to bring my voice to this planet, despite my fears or the DNA I shared with naysayers who told me it wasn't possible. In this book, I share the historical events and my journey, to invite you to find your voice and bring it fully into form.

It has become clear to me that who I am today is a result of my coming to grips with my history as well as the history of my country and the world, honoring my journey, and making choices of personal development and empowerment.

WHAT IS THE VOICE?

When many people think of the word "voice," they think about sound produced in a person's larynx, uttered through the mouth in speech. Others describe it as pitch or tone produced through singing. However you describe it, the voice is about expression, communication, or a proclamation. There is no set way for a voice to be revealed. It is all about a person daring to look at life through the lens of possibility and to live fully expressed.

In this book, we will explore looking at voice from the perspective of the whole. It can be a cultural voice that includes education, institutions, history, or race. We will explore how the voice is used as a tool of engagement. We will also explore how a singular or collective voice enhances empowerment, transparency, and accountability. And finally, we will look at how expression can develop new ideas, shift cultural and political views, transform organizations, create laws, and enhance lives.

The voice can be personal, brought to life in community or through organizations. It can facilitate goals, establish authority, and define rules, objectives, and policies. The voice can share discontent, needs, and desires, which can create great change.

Creativity plays a central role in bringing your voice forward. Here, the forms are endless. Although you may not be conscious of it, in addition to your speaking voice, your authentic voice can also be creatively expressed through music, dance, writing, poetry, clothing, design, art (in all its forms), games, traditional media, social media, marketing, and branding.

WHY DON'T WE HAVE A VOICE?

I believe that every person on this planet wants to feel loved, safe, cared for, and honored. There is a deep need to feel that we have choices and that those choices are respected. Some call these human rights, and these include things such as the right to be educated; the right to have clean water and food sources; the right to practice religion; the right to love whomever you love; the right to live in a safe community; and the right to speak your mind, express your heart, and express your personhood without fear of being harmed for using your voice.

Today, division is playing out around the world. People take sides and refuse to entertain that any other point of view could be reasonable. This separation takes place in families, neighborhoods, communities, politics, and corporations. Judgmental ways of being stop us from remembering that we are on this planet together and ultimately need one another.

We are also living in a time where these rights are often denied. People are forced to live in extreme circumstances in which they are starving, brutalized, fleeing with nothing in hand, and being violated in horrific ways. Families are dying at sea because the only way they see to escape is by getting into unsafe boats and crossing stormy seas. Immigration is overwhelming countries around the world, with overpopulated refugee camps and host countries that cannot manage the influx of wounded souls making their way across the borders. The sense of helplessness and lack of vision for support is present.

The stories are astounding, as children are being recruited to go to war and sold by their families to get money. Girls are raped and disfigured with chemicals thrown into their faces, because the culture does not protect them. Boys and girls alike, incapable of escaping the unwanted advances by ruthless men, lose their safety and security in an instant.

Perhaps even more shocking is the truth that genocide and slavery still exist despite claims otherwise. Entire groups of people are eradicated or imprisoned, forced to submit their will to the demands of others.

And yet, there is hope.

I am living proof that anyone can move out of discord, create a powerful life, and find his or her authentic voice. Today, I coach people around the world, have authored several award-winning books, recorded many music CDs and meditation tapes, and speak on international stages.

Growing up, I thought I was the only one that didn't have a voice. I felt completely alone. I learned quickly that speaking up and speaking out caused pain. My stepfather consistently molested me and beat my mother. I got very good at staying below the radar in my home. When I was six years old, my uncle came with his car. My mother told me to help her, and my uncle put things in a sheet. These were our belongings. We could only take a few things with us. She was trying to move fast, but she was pregnant with my brother, David, and so my hands were needed. We threw the sheet in my uncle's car and left. I would learn later that there was only a one-hour window to get us to safety.

During grade school, we moved a lot, and I had learned to be timid and very insecure. The landlords pursued my mother because she was beautiful and an easy mark. I felt ashamed that we stood in food lines for cheese. I was angry and prone to unexpected outbursts and fights with schoolmates. I felt very much out of control. It was during this time I realized that my entire family was challenged. Grandparents, aunts, uncles, and cousins were all in some sort of dysfunction. The way we all coped varied, but all of us found ways to hide and shut down our authenticity. Drugs, casual sex, and uncontrollable outrage were the norm.

In high school, I learned a new tactic. I got very adept at being charming and likable. I was smart, so I joined the chess club, the debate club, and the school chorus and became secretary of my class. I became a teen model and traveled to different areas for competitions. I got good grades and learned I could excel at school.

I also learned that people liked me, and my popularity grew. This was when I noticed what others would do to cope. Somehow I was a safe haven, and people would turn to me to share their life experiences. I heard stories of alcoholic parents, abuse in the home, husbands and wives who cheated, and mental illness that was being hidden. I didn't know what to say to support them, but I was a great listener and realized that people really want to be heard.

All these stories were secrets, and I realized that I was part of a population of young people and communities that had no voice. We were all afraid to be fully seen, all afraid that someone would find out how crazy our lives were and we would be ostracized. Here is the interesting thing—culture and class didn't matter. This group was white, Black, Asian, and Hispanic. Some were poor, some were middle-class, and some lived in affluent communities.

I didn't know it then, but that was the beginning of the path leading me to do the work I do today.

My deepest desire is that you will use this book to uncover and reveal your authentic voice. Use the stories and exercises to support you in launching an adventure of self-discovery. You are an original imprint, and your voice matters.

HOW TO USE THE BOOK

This book is for anyone who wants to discover the power within that makes you special. That uniqueness is your own glorious way of expressing on this planet, and it is calling you to come out. It doesn't matter if your awakening is large or small. It doesn't matter if it is a growth stretch from something you have already started. And it doesn't matter what your age, race, religion, or history are; anyone can begin right where they are.

Each chapter has three sections. I begin with an overview of the history of that decade. This is by no means an in-depth look at history. It is just an opportunity for you to have an understanding and context of the times. I learned that no matter what age you are, the culture and environment are having impact.

The second part is my story—what I was experiencing at the time and how society, my familial history, and my choices forged the life I live today. Each decade brought me closer to recognizing that I had a voice and how I could use it.

The third section is for you to explore yourself, your identity, and your life choices. It will be an opportunity to connect to your voice and maybe even bring it forward in new ways. I will give you steps that you can do at your own pace. I invite you to get a journal and label it "Finding My Voice." Use it for every exercise in the book. You do not have to share this with anyone unless that is your desire. I promise that there will be powerful insights and revelations.

This is not required, but I encourage you to try it. I have discovered over time, for me and from working with thousands of people, that self-reflection can be a game changer.

Take your time as you travel through my life and see how each decade informed my expression today. My deep desire is that my journey and processes will open portals for your expansive life. As you read this book, use my journey to open up to questions within yourself. Take some time to look at your history from the perspective of "What if?" What if those challenges were opportunities? What if that dream or desire can still be fulfilled? What if my presence on this planet matters? What if nothing is wrong? What if there is nothing to fix? What if everything that has occurred in my life has brought me to this moment? What if I am an integral part of making this world a better place and bringing love into form?

For me, what is important is that we, the culture, wake up and bring our voices and talents into full visibility. My deepest desire is that humanity finds a way to come to the universal table, bringing our varied voices and opinions so that we can learn from each other and remember that we are interconnected.

Our differences are our strengths. Our uniqueness allows for everyone to matter. Then and only then can we work together to create a world that honors all life. Only then will we remember that *all voices matter*.

CHAPTER 1

Born Into Broken Systems

1948

- Mahatma Gandhi is assassinated in India.
- The House Un-American Activities Committee accuses Alger Hiss of spying for the Soviet Union.
- Communists seize power in Czechoslovakia.
- The US Congress ratifies the Marshall Plan, approving $17 billion in European aid.
- The State of Israel is created and admits over two hundred thousand European war refugees.
- The Soviet Union seals off land routes to Berlin; the West responds with a massive airlift of provisions.
- President Harry S. Truman is reelected in an upset over Thomas E. Dewey.
- President Truman integrates the US Armed Forces.
- The World Health Organization is formed by the United Nations.

- Selective Service is inaugurated, providing a continuous peacetime military draft until it is repealed in 1973.
- New York's Idlewild Airport opens (renamed JFK Airport in 1963).
- Swiss outdoorsman George de Mestral invents Velcro.
- Noted food critic Duncan Hines founds a company to make prepackaged cake mixes.

Systems get broken when people stop caring. It seems easier to move into states of denial than to face the challenges before us. We cease to be compassionate, and then we defend our positions. This is a problem that is, and has been, crossing the lines of race, culture, corporations, governments, and religious institutions for centuries.

Modern societies are confronted with the challenges of disappearing natural resources, fierce competition on global markets, and threats of nuclear engagement. Systems that have become outmoded, initially created to solve challenges, are now the problem. Bureaucracy, inept leaders, political conflicts, and non-forward-thinking strategies have organizations in chaos. Children are being abused and tossed from one foster home to another, with no plan on educating and preparing them to live in the world. Drug and mental health issues are out of control, with no clear strategies to shift the challenge. There are consistent calls for people to be released from social services, without training or support to create spaces for enhancing life. Thus poverty and lack of education perpetuate the problems.

The system of families is failing. People feel disconnected and dysfunctional. The family, in many cases, is no longer a place for respite and support. It is a place that people run from, because the lines of communication are broken. The shrinking middle class and the poorer population have been forced into survival mode, which has people overworking or sustaining multiple jobs to stay afloat. The question becomes how families stay honestly present, face the family demons, and consciously shift their thinking.

Corporate systems are failing. Managers do not manage. They oversee and push people to become overwhelmed and overworked. People are treated like numbers and asked to do things that take their integrity. Engagement in workplaces is at an all-time low because people are mistreated and dishonored. People leave jobs because they are not managed or appreciated.

Social services organizations are failing. Social workers are underpaid, people are accepting jobs to survive, training is limited, and caseloads are impossible to handle. Staffing is limited by cost reductions, and complacency permeates the system.

Educational systems are failing. Poor communities lack enthusiastic teachers and up-to-date books and material, and many students lack support at home. First-generation students in college drop out at an alarming rate. Student loans are outrageous, and defaults happen consistently. An archaic system of learning is still being enforced even though research tells us that children and adults learn in a myriad of ways.

The ripple effect of all of this is that the support of human value wanes. We are simply forgetting to honor humanity as a whole. If we valued humans, we would invest in their safety, growth, and education.

I am the product of a broken system. This truth would follow me through decades of my life.

Even as a baby, I felt like I didn't belong. I felt like an alien in my family. My mother would tell stories of me running from her or disappearing in a department store. She would say she was standing right next to me, and then poof, I was gone. I think my soul knew I had to live a better life.

We were on welfare, we moved a lot, and my early childhood was riddled with painful experiences. My biological father was an active alcoholic. He floated in and out of our lives from the time I was born. He married Mom because she was pregnant but left us very soon after my birth. When I was around a year and a half, he would show up periodically and take me to his favorite bar and have me dance for the people. When Mom found out, she was livid and put a stop to it. For the longest time, he was only allowed to see me at home. Then he would disappear for large periods of time.

There was something in me that defied my surroundings. We lived with my grandmother for a while, and there are stories of me crying for no reason. The only thing that would calm me down was being put in this antique chair that had lions' heads and paws. Somehow when they put me in the chair, I would instantly stop crying. My grandmother used to say that I could feel the ancestors. She willed that chair to me when she died, and it still sits in my office. I agree with her about the ancestors. I still feel a calming energy when I look at the chair or sit in it.

Mom had to work, so she left me a lot with my uncle Dan and his wife. I loved my uncle. I can still remember sitting on his lap as an infant and feeling so connected. That was not the case with his wife. For some reason, she didn't like me. When she was asked to care for me, she would lock me in the basement and tell me the boogeyman was going to get me. It took my mother months to get me to stop screaming when I was near the basement door. She told me that one day I fell on the floor screaming that the boogeyman was going to eat me. She was calm enough to ask how I knew that, and I told her. This set off a huge fight. My uncle protected his wife, and soon we moved out. The details of where we went and how we lived are foggy. Today I understand that my mom was keeping me safe, even though it meant hardship for her.

Children don't know that they are living challenging lives. They only see, know, and understand the circumstances of their current reality. It is only when they get exposed to different life experiences that they begin to understand that they are not like others. Then they have a choice. Which path will they choose to move forward—more of the same, or will they step into the unknown and create something new?

I was always a creative. Mom would tell, in horror, the story of my performing for the insurance man. He was in our living room going over options with Mom. At age three, I came singing and dancing down the stairs. I had her bra on my head and was wearing a crazy outfit I had thrown together from her drawer. Mom was mortified. The insurance man thought I was cute. He was a great audience, and even though Mom was telling me to go upstairs, I was delighted to be a performer. Something in me knew I was destined to be on stage, and I was not going to obey Mom—not while I had someone willing to listen and cheer me on.

I believe our call is to create the invitation and wherewithal for people to heal the hurts and tear down the fences of separation. It can start as a seed within a child and blossom into the manifestation of a fulfilled life. That seed can become something powerful and amazing. The only thing required to nurture it is a fierce determination to shift the current reality and create new ways of being. *People in broken systems can surrender to suffering* or *activate courage.* Every time someone holds a new vision, makes an empowering decision, and moves into action, the possibility for new and empowering systems comes to life.

The broken systems then and now block the flow of possibility for people that want to make a difference. They keep people locked in paradigms that deepen fear and perpetuate a scarcity mentality. These systems communicate that there is no hope. Well, I don't agree, and if I can move out of that way of thinking, others can do the same.

Our call as a human race is to create both the invitation and the stamina to help people to heal their hurts and tear down the fences of separation.

▶ *Exercise for the reader:*

The exercises in this chapter will take you on an exploration of your childhood and the beliefs that have held or hold you hostage. Here we begin an exploration into the dreams that were thwarted and the decisions that were made that stopped you from living a life that was truly vital and thriving. I invite you to get a journal and label it "Finding My Voice." Use it for every exercise in the book. Only share if it feels supportive. This book is for you.

▶ LET'S GET REAL

Where did you come from? What was your early childhood like? What were the familial messages that were undeniable? What challenged you the most? What did you or your family do to survive? Getting these things out will open the portal for new beginnings.

▶ WHAT'S YOUR DREAM?

Now that you have shared your past, I invite you to take a moment and write down, stream of consciousness, what your ideal life would look like. You don't have to know how to get there. Make it specific! What are you doing that ignites passion within you? Where would you like to live? What kind of people do you want in your life? Do you want a family? Do you want to travel? Don't hold back.

Dream big! This exercise can be the beginning of a breakthrough that moves you out of old systems that do not support your freedom and expression. We will do more of this.

CHAPTER 2

Everything Starts with a Call

THE '50s
During this decade, the world continued its recovery from World War II, aided by the post–World War II economic expansion.

It was the dawn of the Cold War and the emerging of the civil rights movement in the United States. Lots of things were happening, and much focus was on the following:

- The Diners Club issues the first credit cards.
- Famous physicist Albert Einstein warns the world that nuclear war would lead to mutual destruction.
- The United States develops and produces *I Love Lucy* on the CBS network.
- The United States ratifies the Twenty-Second Amendment, limiting a president to two terms.
- The first hydrogen bomb is successfully detonated by the United States.

- Puerto Rico is named as a self-governing commonwealth of the United States.
- Jonas Salk develops the first polio vaccine.
- The first James Bond novel, *Casino Royale*, is published by British author Ian Fleming.
- The US Supreme Court rules that racial segregation is unconstitutional in public schools in their unanimous decision of Brown v. Board of Education.
- US senator Joseph McCarthy is censured by the Senate, ending his four-year-long hunt for Communists within the US government.
- Frozen TV dinners are introduced by Swanson.
- *The Mickey Mouse Club* premieres. The Disneyland theme park in California opens.
- Rosa Parks is arrested in Alabama after she refuses to give up her bus seat to a white passenger, sparking the civil rights movement.
- Albert Sabin creates the oral polio vaccine to replace the Salk vaccine.
- Nine African American students enroll at Little Rock Central High School in Arkansas and are met with resistance by protesters and the state's governor. Federal troops end up escorting the students into the school at the command of President Eisenhower.
- The National Aeronautics and Space Administration (NASA) is created.
- The Cuban Revolution ends and Fidel Castro comes to power, creating the first Communist nation in the West.
- Alaska and Hawaii are admitted as the forty-ninth and fiftieth states in the United States.

Every change in the individual and the collective begins with a call to investigate discomfort, inequality, injustice, and a need to do or be something more.

This was a time when women were changing roles. Their duties were primarily as wives and mothers, but they also worked outside of the home and made up a significant portion of the postwar labor force. There were many television shows depicting women as the perfect, sometimes odd, and subservient wife and mother: *The Adventures of Ozzie and Harriet*, *The Honeymooners*, *I Love Lucy*, and *Father Knows Best*. We watched the shows and would laugh that our mothers didn't look or act that way. There were no people of color; it was like we didn't exist. It was also clear that the shows were telling women how to act and about the lifestyles we should all seek to attain. However, the 1950s were also the beginning of changes in sexual behavior, which would lead to the sexual revolution of the 1960s. I will talk more about that in the next chapter.

There was a growing group of Americans speaking out against inequality and injustice. Brown v. Board of Education went to the Supreme Court, and it was declared that "separate educational facilities" for Black children were "inherently unequal." Many southern whites resisted the Brown ruling. They withdrew their children from public schools and enrolled them in all-white "segregation academies" and used violence and intimidation to prevent Blacks from asserting their rights. In 1956 more than one hundred southern congressmen even signed a Southern Manifesto declaring that they would do all they could to defend segregation.

In December of 1955 a Montgomery activist named Rosa Parks was arrested for refusing to give up her seat on a city bus to a white person. Her arrest sparked a thirteen-month boycott of the city's buses by its Black citizens, which only ended when the bus companies stopped discriminating against African American passengers. Acts of nonviolent resistance such as the boycott helped shape the civil rights movement of the next decade. I thought she was brave but could not see myself as being that courageous in my own life. At the time, it seemed crazy to put one's life at risk on this level.

There was a lot of conversation about the suburbs. At the end of World War II, veterans returned home; they had families and needed places to live. The housing industry was growing in the 1950s, as the federal government subsidized mass-production builders to create suburbs on the condition that those homes be sold only to whites. I was aware that many of the white families were moving to the suburbs because they were not so happy about the diversity in schools. However, it didn't seem like a big deal. I loved being where I was and having so many friends of different races.

I was young in the 1950s, but I began to notice conversations in my family that seemed confusing. My family kept saying they moved north to avoid some of the insanity we were witnessing in the South. We had just gotten a television and were watching Black people being beaten and children barred from entering schools. My family told me that Black people were fighting for rights and to have a voice in our nation. No one seemed to think it was going to make a difference, but they were happy that some were trying. It felt weird and scary. I couldn't understand why people would put themselves in dangerous circumstances to achieve their goals, especially if so many didn't think it would fix the problem. It was hard enough for us to live and for me to support my brother while Mom worked. Having a drunk for a father who showed up periodically—and having escaped an abusive life with my stepfather—was more than enough to let me know that safety was the most important thing in life.

I grew up on welfare. We lived in dark, cold apartments in unsafe neighborhoods. My mother was a proud woman, and as a single mother of two, she was unwilling to let us starve or be laughed at because of our clothes. She fought to keep her dignity as men tried to convince her to let them be her savior. We consistently moved from one place to another, as she refused to be bought. I didn't understand what was happening, but I was clear that my mother was beautiful and men, many of them distasteful, wanted to be in her company. We kept our doors locked and were told to never, under any circumstances, let anyone in when she was not home. There was this underlying sadness that Mom carried. She felt judged and often commented on the hopelessness she experienced. Many years later, we would discuss the guilt she carried. She shared how many people looked down on us because we got "handouts." I knew we were strapped for money and always robbing Peter to pay Paul. Early one morning, Mom woke us up in a panic. The house was on fire. The landlord was drunk and fell asleep with a cigarette in his hand. Mom wrapped us in blankets, and we got out just in time. In that moment, she made a decision that things had to change.

The welfare income didn't pay the bills or take care of us, so Mom did something illegal. She got a job under an assumed name and worked nights from 11:00 p.m. to 7:00 a.m. Today that could not happen, but somehow it worked for her. I was left alone with my young brother and took care of us both. Mom would come home in the morning, make sure we had breakfast, and get us off to school. Then she would sleep until we came home. She would oversee homework and make dinner. She would rest again before she left for work. She made just enough to make sure we lived in a clean, safe space; paid the rent and bills; and kept food on the table. She often complained of being tired and worried. We weren't rich, but we seemed fine. Today, I realize that her sacrifices were to make sure that my brother and I had a better life.

My cousins were in similar situations. There were twelve of us, and we lived close to one another in the same neighborhood. We would play together, create silly talent shows, and often got in trouble for playing in ways that could challenge the family. One night the cousins decided to take a bath together. We were having fun. We were throwing water and laughing. All of a sudden, my aunt Ruth burst into the bathroom and started yelling. She turned off the water and made us all get out of the tub and line up according to our size. Evidently the water was leaking into the living room downstairs. We got spanked with a towel while we were still naked and wet. It wasn't funny at the time, but later in life we laughed about it, because those were the days we all felt connected.

My aunts and uncle could not have been any more different. My aunt Ruth was a sexy beauty. She was bold and brash and didn't care what others thought. She flirted and danced whenever we were together or had a community gathering, making sure all the men in the vicinity noticed her beautiful bottom. My aunt Mickey was a tall, elegant woman. She was very smart but insecure. We saw her marry and remarry a man that abused her terribly and dared anyone to intervene. My uncle Dan lived close, but he and his family kept a little distance. In retrospect it was probably wise. There was a lot of drama as the sisters navigated the waters of family, relationships, and work life.

Many of my cousins struggled in school and lived through some pretty violent experiences. Gangs were starting to form, and drinking and drugging began to infiltrate our community. School was a real dichotomy. On the one hand there was a lot of diversity. Black, white, Hispanic, and Asian kids hung out together. Of course, there were cliques, but even those groups had diversity. The interesting thing is that I don't remember the majority of teachers inviting us to expand our horizons through education. We either did well or we didn't. I am not sure how I managed to get good grades, except that I have a great memory and learned quickly. Because of the challenges at home, I didn't always study, but I was superb at testing, especially in English, history, French, and music. I also joined clubs. It was primarily because I wanted to get out of doing a bunch of chores at home. I joined the chess club and debate team and became secretary of my class. It placed me in environments with smart kids who wanted to become something in their lives. It was a glimmer of possibility.

I was tired and oftentimes felt resentful that I had to be a parent while my mom worked. When I came home from school activities, we would eat, do homework, and get ready for bed. We did not have real family time, and we had no money to do things we saw television families do. I remember dreaming about someday having a real family—one in which we talked, laughed, and did stuff together. I wanted a normal family life. Today I realize that *Leave It to Beaver*, *Father Knows Best*, *Lassie*, *The Donna Reed Show*, and *The Adventures of Ozzie and Harriet* had nothing to do with reality.

There was a saving grace. Many people in our community were in the same situation. None of my friends lived those television lives. They had their own struggles trying to keep their heads above water. We connected with each other at school, on the phone, and sometimes on the weekends. Those moments were stabilizing for me.

Looking back, I can see that the way we lived was a precursor to what many families are experiencing today. I didn't know I was living in a system that was broken and unsupportive. It was just the way life was. I either found a way to escape the reality that engulfed me or I surrendered to the mundane, unsatisfying existence that I witnessed all around me. It was normal that many of us were what we now call "latchkey kids." It was normal that eight-to-ten-year-olds were the responsible parties when Mom or Dad were working. It was normal that kids got into trouble, because they had no supervision.

Everything Starts with a Call

Minnesota had integrated schools in the inner city, and my mother was clear that education was an entry into freedom. I felt okay in school and couldn't understand the challenge, in our country, with all people going to the same school. I had friends that where Black, white, and Asian. My only disappointment came from being excluded from the cliques of wealthier kids that wore designer clothes. It didn't dawn on me at the time—they were all white. I just wanted to be part of the "cool" group.

When I was in middle school, there was an announcement about an upcoming posture contest. Somehow I was invited to participate. I was reluctant because we had to wear a swimsuit, but my vision of being a star was in the back of my mind. My mother promised to help me pick the perfect one. We went shopping, and a beautiful yellow one-piece caught my eye. It fit perfectly, with one exception. I was flat-chested, and the bra cup sank in. The saleswoman convinced my mother that we needed a small insert. I wasn't convinced, because there was a distinct difference in the look of my chest and how it looked in this swimsuit. Both women said I looked great. I gave in.

The day of the contest came, and I walked out on the stage. I was poised, and I have to admit, I felt pretty. I stood. I walked. I felt confident. The shy part of me, who I refer to as "Cyndi," was nowhere to be seen. I turned and posed, and the room cheered. Clearly I was a hit. The teachers lined us up to announce the winners. One teacher smiled and said, "And the grand champion is Cynthia James." I couldn't believe it—I'd won, even with the false breast inserts. I was elated. Maybe it was okay to be seen.

That swimsuit became my badge of acceptance. The powerful part of me, who I refer to as "Cynthia," was out, and she was grand. Of course, I wanted to go to the beach and show off. I lived in Minneapolis, Minnesota, and there are many lakes. I wanted to go to Calhoun Beach, because it was the place where all the cool people went. I laid my blanket down and strolled out to the water and waded in. I knew how to swim; swimming was required in our school. However, I didn't want to rush in. I wanted people to see how fabulous I looked.

With the water up to my waist, I did my best casual-but-elegant sidestroke. I was poetry in motion. I dove beneath the surface, and when I came up, both inserts popped out of my suit and floated away from me. I tried to get them before anyone could see, but it was too late. People around me began to laugh. There was no way to pretend they weren't mine. I was mortified. The more I tried to get them, the more they slipped away. Finally, I got both and stuffed them back in so I could swim back to shore. People giggled as I picked up my blanket and walked away with my head bowed. This was not a fun experience. As I walked away, I remember saying to myself, *This is just a moment. You won the contest.* That moment anchored within me that "I might be able to get out of the ghetto" mentality. When I look back, many of my family members, friends, and neighbors did not have that kind of conviction. They simply surrendered to the fact that they were poor, had to struggle, and were destined to live painful lives.

That moment in time, that experience, was foundational for me. It planted a seed within me that I could win. It showed me that there were two distinct energies inside of me. One was a child that had been traumatized and abused. She was timid, insecure, and afraid to be visible and bring her voice forward. She was terrified of being hurt. I called her "Cyndi." But there was also a child that was fierce. She had an adventurous spirit. She stepped out, took risks, and pushed boundaries. She was the "Cynthia" I would become. My greatest task in life was to give voice to Cynthia and allow her to create, contribute, and manifest success. I allowed her brave spirit to guide me into the unknown and open portals of possibility. She would be the key to finding my voice.

The junior high school I attended had a swimming pool, and it was mandatory to swim. For me and every other Black girl, this created trauma. Our hair did not do well in water. It became nappy. For those of you who don't understand that term, it is when African American hair reverts to its natural state—some call it "kinky."

During that time, we worked hard to prevent our hair from shrinking up and getting tight on our heads. "Nappy-headed" meant we didn't look good to white people. The term was originally created to describe how slaves' hair looked. The negative use of "nappy" referenced tightly curled hair. As time progressed, the terminology changed, but the judgment did not. Afros, dreadlocks, and other styles of coarse-textured African hair always seemed like an albatross until African Americans decided to reclaim their natural style.

Honoring your natural hair was not the style when I was in school. I wore two swimming caps to make sure my hair did not get wet. We were not allowed to wear hats or scarves in school, so I was determined to keep my hair looking straight. This was no easy task. My mother either pressed my hair with a hot comb or relaxed it with a straightener made of lye. This burned and took all the life out of my hair.

My hair was not as coarse as some. It was a blend of my mother's curly hair and my father's super-tight curl. So when it was pressed or relaxed, the hair just lay flat on my head. If I was in humidity or rain, it blew up and got wild. The products for Black hair were designed for coarser hair, so it was a big challenge for my mother to keep me looking presentable.

One day I was in the pool, and the class was about to end. I was told to dive in one more time. I was nervous because I was not a great diver. I got out of the water and went to the side of the pool. I dove in, and the unspeakable happened. Both of my swimming caps came off, and my hair was drenched. I was mortified. The other Black girls in the pool were speechless. I slowly got out of the water and quietly walked to my teacher. I whispered that I needed a pass to go home to fix my hair. I only lived a few blocks away and could be back in thirty to forty minutes. The teacher looked at me, smirked, and said, "Absolutely not!"

I tried to keep my composure, but I was starting to panic. I pleaded, "Please—I don't want the others to make fun of me!"

She just turned and walked away as she said, "Get dressed and get to your next class. This is the end of this discussion." The other Black girls felt sorry for me but didn't dare say a word.

This was a choice point. I was a "good" girl. I followed the rules. I helped Mom around the house and supported my brother. But in this instance, I was angry and scared at the same time. I could stay in school and be ridiculed, or go home and take whatever punishment would come. I chose the latter. I ran home, pressed my hair, and put it in a bun. My mom wasn't home, so she had no idea. When I got back to school, I had to go to the office to get a pass to get back in class. The principal had no sympathy and sent me home. He told me not to come back until my mother came with me.

I was enraged, upset, and dreading talking to my mother. When she got home from work, I meekly entered her room and told her what happened. I was prepared for her to scream and yell. Instead she said, "Why did you choose to come home?"

I told her I was clear that the teacher did not understand or care about my predicament or the impact of water on my hair. I was unwilling to be laughed at and ridiculed by the students. I knew it would not be a one-time thing. The humiliation would last for a long time. She looked at me and only said, "I see."

The next day we went to school early. We sat in the chairs outside of the principal's office. I was nervous and terrified. I wanted my mother's approval. She sat there calmly. This was unusual. My mother was a worrier and usually quite emotional.

Finally, we were told to go in. We sat down, and the principal declared, "Your daughter was out of line. She was told not to go home, and she went anyway. This is unacceptable behavior. I really should suspend her."

My mother waited for him to finish, and then she said, "Do you have any idea how hard it is to be a teenager? How hard it is to be a colored girl in this school? My daughter is not a rebel. She is an A student and engages in many extra activities. Our hair is different than yours. That is not the challenge. The problem is that when it gets wet, it responds differently than yours, and children are not always kind. To have your hair shrink up and be unmanageable sets colored girls up to be humiliated and laughed at incessantly. My daughter only wanted forty-five minutes to look presentable. She exercised her right to take care of herself. I don't see that she had a choice."

I was stunned. Apparently so was the principal. He was quiet. Then he said, "I will not suspend her, but she will have to do several days of after-school detention."

My mother said, "If that is the price for standing up for herself, then that is what it will have to be." She thanked him, the principal gave me a pass to go to class, and Mom walked me to the classroom. She smiled, kissed me on the cheek, and whispered in my ear, "I'm proud of you. I don't like disobedience, but standing up for yourself sometimes is what's necessary." Then she just walked away, and we never spoke of it again.

I didn't realize it at the time, but she was teaching me that finding my voice and standing up for myself was needed for me to be successful in life. In retrospect, this was surprising. My mother mostly felt like a victim and had a hard time finding her voice. How incredible that, in that moment, she found a way to stand up for me.

It took me quite a while to speak up for myself again, because I truly did not know how to navigate the waters of being a woman of color in a nation that did not honor my presence, race, or gender. I knew that I was not going to live my life in Minnesota, because I had a deep desire to see the world. How I was going to get there was another matter. I do believe that the pool incident was the beginning of a call for me to play bigger in my life. Somehow I discovered a place of dignity within myself that would not take no for an answer.

You have a calling. You are an original imprint. There is no one like you on the planet, and there is something inside of you that wants to emerge. Some call it a dream or a deep desire. Whatever you call it, something wants to come through you and take form. It doesn't have to be a huge thing. Not everyone is Mahatma Gandhi, Mother Teresa, or Martin Luther King Jr. But we are all here for a reason. The work becomes listening to that inner call, trusting it, and moving into action.

I believe that callings come in different forms and at different stages in life. Every shift in my existence began with an inner nudge or a situation that I could not avoid. I didn't always listen, and struggle often ensued. If there is a calling, there is a delivery system. Most of us have not been taught this, so we wander through life until clarity is realized. Make no mistake, your presence on Earth is significant. You matter, and what you must do or say is needed. The question becomes whether you are willing to listen to the call and move in the direction of your dreams and desires beyond adversity.

▶ *Exercise for the reader:*

This is an invitation to move into discovery.

▶ REMEMBERING MOMENTS

Write down a minimum of five incidents in your childhood in which you stood up for yourself or maybe even became a rebel. Some of you will have vivid memories, and for others it will take a little longer. Maybe you ran away from home, stole a cookie from the cookie jar that your family thought they hid, pushed back on a bully, refused to wear an awful outfit your mother thought was great, told your sibling to back off, or refused to go out with someone your family loved. Whatever it is, large or small, don't discount it.

It could be an experience or situation in which you felt dismissed, unseen, unheard. It could be a circumstance in which you felt disempowered and withdrew your energy. It could also be a moment in which you stood up for yourself, no matter the consequence. Be aware of what was going on in your world, your community, or your family and how it may have impacted your behavior.

In those moments, you answered a call to be your authentic self. It may not have been rewarded, but it did plant seeds. Here are a few of mine:

- I stood up for myself in the pool incident about my hair.
- I hit and pushed Arthur (a nerdy boy in third grade) after he tried to kiss me in the cloakroom—ugh.
- I yelled at my stepfather to stop hitting my mother.

- I told my cousins to back off when they made fun of my dreams to be a singer. I was clear I was going to make it, no matter what they said.
- I told my grandmother how upset I was when she killed my pet chicken to make dinner for the family. She told me we needed to eat, and I told her I didn't care and that she had no right to kill my friend.
- I talked back to my father, who had dropped in unannounced, was drunk, and was telling me what to do. I told him a father is present and keeps his word.
- I wrote in my journal about unfair situations and told people off in my words. They might never see them, but it felt great to push back.

Recalling these moments will remind you that you always had a voice, whether people listened or not.

Don't judge this process. Each exercise will build on the next. I'm excited to walk through this journey with you.

CHAPTER 3

Life's Challenges:
An Invitation To Create

THE '60s

As the call for human rights was evolving, many areas were touched. College student activism, community activism, the Black Arts Movement, and calls to action burst on the scene. We were no longer able to pretend that the cultural divide wasn't real.

The 1960s were iconic. Revolutions started, art erupted, and we were able to see some of the most incredible feats in human achievement that would create the lives we live today:

- Democrat John F. Kennedy wins the US presidential election after defeating Republican Richard Nixon.
- Alan Shepard becomes the first American in space.
- Construction on the Berlin Wall begins in an effort to separate East and West Berlin.

- The Bay of Pigs invasion is an unsuccessful US-backed operation to overthrow Fidel Castro in Cuba.
- The Peace Corps is created.
- The Cuban Missile Crisis has the world on the edge of another world war as the United States and the USSR come close to launching nuclear attacks.
- James Meredith becomes the first African American student to enroll at the University of Mississippi.
- The comic book character of Spider-Man makes his debut in the *Amazing Fantasy* #15 comic.
- The Beatles release their first single, "Love Me Do," in the United Kingdom.
- President John F. Kennedy is assassinated by Lee Harvey Oswald.
- US civil rights leader Martin Luther King Jr. gives his famous "I Have a Dream" speech.
- The United States begins to use zip codes.
- US president Lyndon B. Johnson signs the Civil Rights Act of 1964 into law.
- NASA's *Mariner 4* space probe successfully approaches Mars and becomes the first spacecraft to take images of a planet from deep space.
- Sidney Poitier wins the Academy Award for Best Actor, becoming the first Black actor to win that honor.
- The Voting Rights Act is signed into law by President Lyndon Johnson.
- Martin Luther King Jr. leads a peaceful civil rights march from Selma to Montgomery in Alabama.
- The Vietnam War escalates, and opposition to it begins to mount as anti-Vietnam protests become more common.
- The first episode of the popular television show *Star Trek* airs.

- *Rolling Stone* publishes its first magazine issue.
- Thurgood Marshall is appointed to the Supreme Court, becoming the first African American Supreme Court justice.
- Civil rights leader Martin Luther King Jr. is assassinated in April of 1968 by James Earl Ray.
- The Civil Rights Act of 1968 is signed into law by President Johnson.
- Richard Nixon wins the US presidential election.
- Neil Armstrong and Buzz Aldrin become the first men to go to the moon.
- The Woodstock music festival takes place in New York and features such acts as Janis Joplin, Jimi Hendrix, Jefferson Airplane, and the Who.
- The popular children's television show *Sesame Street* debuts.
- Cassius Clay defeats Sonny Liston, later becoming known as "Muhammad Ali."

Flower power erupted, and young people declared a need for free love. The Black Arts Movement was born. This movement was comprised of politically motivated Black poets, artists, dramatists, musicians, and writers who emerged in the wake of the Black Power movement.

In 1961 the Bay of Pigs invasion of Cuba became a disastrous attempt to topple the Communist regime of Fidel Castro, and in 1962 President Kennedy faced down the Kremlin in the Cuban Missile Crisis as the superpowers stood at the precipice of nuclear war. My family believed Kennedy was going to be a savior for our country. Then in 1963 he was assassinated, and the country was devastated. I was in my choir class when the news of the shooting was announced. The entire school wept. It felt like hope was gone. Our community was very upset that

Lyndon Johnson was now our president. He was from Texas, and people were wary.

Johnson wanted, what he called, a "Great Society" for all Americans. He championed Medicare, Head Start, the Voting Rights Act, and the Civil Rights Act. These programs would have a profound and lasting impact on health, education, and civil rights. At the same time, Johnson's legacy was challenged by his failure to lead the nation out of the Vietnam War. Oftentimes people don't know how to navigate big, uncomfortable change. This was one of those times.

Martin Luther King Jr. was rising to prominence. He had a powerful voice and invited African American people to take a peaceful stand. His vision of humanity united gave rise to possibility. And then he, too, was killed.

Thousands of anti-war, antiestablishment demonstrators clashed with police at the Democratic National Convention in Chicago. This sent televised images of violence and anger to the world and raised the possibility that America was undergoing a nervous breakdown. Stokely Carmichael spoke at the Student Nonviolent Coordinating Committee (SNCC) and coined the phrase "Black Power."

I, along with family and friends, felt like we were on an emotional roller coaster. Many were becoming afraid to leave home. It felt dangerous, and no one knew how to navigate the murky waters.

All the while, a growing youth rebellion caught fire, and Richard Nixon, a conservative, was inaugurated as president. My community went nuts. There was no trust in Nixon, and people felt like their rights were doomed.

North Minneapolis was known as a place where marginalized people came together. Restrictive housing covenants prevented both Jewish and African American citizens from buying homes elsewhere in Minneapolis, so Northside became an area where residents from different backgrounds cooperated, built friendships, and even intermarried.

On the night of July 19, 1967, racial tension in North Minneapolis erupted along Plymouth Avenue in the form of arson, assaults, and vandalism. The violence, which lasted for three nights, is often linked with other race-related demonstrations in cities across the nation during 1967's "long, hot summer."

The anti-war movement emerged as the Black Power movement emphasized racial pride, economic empowerment, and the creation of political and cultural institutions for Black people in the United States.

The conflict of the country lived within me and within my community. How were we going to survive if the American people could not honor one another and reveal peace with ourselves and other countries? I made the choice, like many others in my life, to keep my head down and find ways to take care of myself. I decided to become visible through my gifts.

Throughout history, artists on every level have been change agents. Within each of us is an artist who wants to express him- or herself. Oftentimes creations come through crisis. In those moments, people journal, draw, sing, dance, and bring to life their innermost feelings. This experience births musicians, playwrights, authors, journalists, athletes, photographers, and activists, all of whom take bold steps.

Artistry was still on the rise in 1969, and nearly a half million young people gathered that summer on a six-hundred-acre farm in New York for the Woodstock festival. This was a three-day concert and celebration of music, peace, and love that they hoped would demonstrate a new way of living for the future. Around the same time, The Harlem Cultural Festival was filled with stars from soul, R&B, blues and jazz and drew more than 300,000 people. They got no media coverage.

Outer conflict is always a mirror of inner conflict. This is true for individuals, communities, and nations. Many people look at challenges as mountains that cannot be climbed. What if each conflict was just an invitation? Or, maybe, a call to shift our thinking and our behaviors?

HIGH SCHOOL AND MY EMERGING

Let me start here by saying I wasn't confident, but I was good at hiding it. I had been quiet and shy as a child and quickly learned that the more extroverted people got positive attention. My teen years were tumultuous and mirrored what was happening in my family and the country. There were times I felt optimistic, and other times I was in the throes of uncertainty. I was looking for my identity and floundered on many levels. Just like the rest of the country, I was looking for my voice, a feeling of safety, and a way to express myself. This was a time of extremes. I was aware that a part of me wanted to bring my creativity forward, but I didn't know how. Another part wanted to stay below the radar for safety. I was in my early teens when my grandmother, Mama, took me to see plays with Black actors, and a spark was born. I began to think that maybe, just maybe, I could bring my talents to the stage.

Our family didn't have money and couldn't afford to buy great clothes. My mother and grandmother made a lot of what I wore because we were barely off welfare. I knew I had to get creative if I was going to survive high school. I joined the debate team and became good at learning how to persuade people that my logic was strong. We traveled to different schools, and I got a reputation as a great debater. As mentioned earlier, I was elected secretary of my class and got selected to be a teen model at a department store. All of this was unusual for an African American. I felt that the more I accomplished, the easier it would be to escape the craziness of my heritage. I stayed away from political conversations. My visibility was growing, but the place where I really shone was through my singing.

The fact that people liked my voice was curious to me. Aretha Franklin, Gladys Knight, and the Motown people were hot, and my voice was nothing like any of theirs. I was in the choir, and that seemed like a good place for me. I could hide there and still feel accomplished. All of this mattered if I had any chance of going to college. Somehow I was continuously asked to do solos. It was scary, but I remember thinking that if I was popular, life would be good.

Singing also brought the attention of boys. I was tall and skinny and nothing like the cute, curvy girls. I wasn't ready for sex, so I'm sure I seemed boring. The saving grace was there were several boys at my church who thought I was cute. They also liked to hear me sing.

When I was fifteen years old, Anthony Roberts really liked me. He would ride his bike to my house, and I would talk to him from the kitchen window. It felt so romantic. He was very handsome and so sweet. I just knew he was going to be my boyfriend. We didn't go to the same school, but he liked my voice and really wanted us to connect. My mother was not having it. She told me I was too young for a boyfriend and told him not to come back. I was devastated and felt clear she was ruining my life. I didn't deal with boys again until I was seventeen. I had crushes but spoke about none of them.

Minneapolis had many dance places for teens. They had live bands, and kids of all races would gather there on the weekends. One of the bands was hot—they had a duo that sounded like the Righteous Brothers, and people flocked to see them. One of the band members heard me sing and asked me to join the band. At first, I was surprised and couldn't understand why they wanted me. They told me I was perfect, and I would get paid seventy-five dollars a week. Wow! I ran home and asked my mom. She wanted to meet the band members and see if it was legitimate. Somehow they convinced her they would take care of me, and she said yes.

Singing in that band gave me great joy. I loved learning new things and stretching as a singer. I also loved the attention. We played often at two clubs, Magoo's and Mr. Lucky's, on Nicollet Avenue and Lake Street. A girl in a band was unique, so we got a lot of attention.

One night I was singing, and I saw one of the most beautiful boys I had ever seen. He was white, tall, lean, and gorgeous. I couldn't take my eyes off him. Later, I saw my cousin Stephen talking to him. I trusted my cousin and asked him to introduce me. He obliged, told me his name was Steve Johnson, and introduced us. It was totally uneventful. Steve didn't seem the least bit interested. For some reason, I was super disappointed.

Later that night, after the gig, people gathered at a drive-in to eat hamburgers. This was a ritual. Music blared in cars, and kids hung out and talked. I was sitting in a car, and someone walked to my window. I heard a voice say, "Hello, princess." I looked up and it was Steve. My heart pounded, and I was sure he could hear. We talked and he asked for my number. I was certain this was love at first sight and that I was going to marry him and have his children.

Our love affair was powerful and lasted for a year. He was a poet, smart, and the first to introduce me to loving sexuality. He was gentle and attentive and made me feel safe. My mother liked him, but I was scared about his parents. That turned out to be the least of my worries. One day he told me that he had my picture up in his room, and his mom asked who I was. He simply said, "My girlfriend."

He had my attention. I asked, "Well, what did she say?"

He said, "She smiled and said you were pretty." Whoa—this was so cool. It was one more thing that made me feel this was destiny.

First loves can be so powerful. Usually, they awaken within us something we didn't know existed. That kind of love is free, honoring, and filled with passion and wide-open hearts. I don't know about you, but when I look back on that moment, it is clear to me that all my defenses were down. Think about your first love. Does it bring a smile to your face, even if it didn't end well? I believe that first loves are portals to a sense of being alive that is unprecedented. It is an invitation to love ourselves.

I was about to be a senior, and my life was incredible. Four girls were renting a house and asked me to be a roommate. My mother freaked out, but I was a debater. I made a great case and asked her to trust me. I was an A student on the honor roll, was really engaged in school activities, was making more than enough money to pay my rent, and had never been in trouble. I told her that if I screwed up at all, I would come home. Somehow she reluctantly agreed. She reminded me of our sex talk and told me to be careful. I understood what she meant. When I was fifteen, she had sat me down, and we had an authentic conversation. She told me that if I needed to have sex, to let her know, and we would get some sort of birth control. That conversation is vivid. She was adamant that a baby would stop me in my tracks, especially because I believed I was head over heels in love. Plus, Steve was hot and gorgeous. There was no way we were not going to have sex.

I moved in, got birth control, went to school, and sang in the band. Steve came over all the time, but I wasn't aware of something. His friends and ex-girlfriend did not like the fact that he had a colored girlfriend. They kept working on him to remember how dangerous my people could be. I didn't know that, but something in me began to feel insecure. I did everything in my power to be "perfect" for him. Looking back, I was clingy and so needy that it had to be annoying. Whatever he liked,

I liked. Whatever he wanted to do, I wanted to do. I even tried to write poetry. I sucked, but he was kind.

The band got a gig in Aspen, Colorado, and it was a big deal. I was so excited. The members of the band had kept their word and took really good care of me. They were protective and made sure I was always safe. One time, when I got drunk on Everclear and Kool-Aid (a sweet and horrible combination), they covered for me and made sure no one took advantage.

Off we went to Aspen. We had a great time, and I bought Steve and myself cool puzzle rings. I couldn't wait to give him his when I returned.

The night I got back, he came over and was acting weird. I was trying to be upbeat, but I was really scared. He told me I was a "great" girl, but our relationship wasn't right. I thought I was going to die. I asked why. He shuffled his feet and looked at the ground. He was vague and couldn't wait to leave. I felt like my life was walking out the door. I must have sobbed for three days.

It wasn't until weeks later that I found out he had gone back to his old girlfriend. They had a lot in common, including drugs. In retrospect, I don't know why I never knew he had a drug issue. He was very good at hiding it, and I was naive. As time went on, there was a series of men in my life with addictive personalities. I will talk more about that later.

Denial is a potent elixir. It blinds us to the fact that the signs for all disconnect are right in front of us. Who wants to see deception, deceit, or inappropriate behavior? No one. We all want to believe what we want to believe, so we turn our backs on signs of betrayal, addiction, or lies. It never ends well, but fantasy thinking is powerful.

I finally recovered, but something within me was damaged. I had worked hard to be a cheerleader and had made the team. I was told that if I missed three practices, I was out. I'm not sure why, but I managed to miss three and was demoted to backup. It was clearly self-sabotage, but I couldn't seem to get my emotions under control.

Steve stayed away from me and my gigs. It was a gift. I licked my wounds by partying a little too much. I also made the decision to do whatever was necessary to get out of Minneapolis and see the world. I was determined that my gender, the color of my skin, and world events were not going to get in my way. Like Martin Luther King Jr., I had a dream.

I wanted to go to college, but we didn't have any money. I got a job at night doing data entry and went to Augsburg College during the day. It was grueling. I hardly had any sleep, but somehow my grades were okay. I left the data job and got a job in a hospital, close to school, as an aide. I was assigned to the psych ward, and it was uncomfortable. Still, it was a way to pay for school, and since my grandmother had been a nurse, I had a good bedside manner and some sense of how to take care of myself.

I stuck it out for one and a half years but began to have meltdowns. I couldn't keep burning the candle at both ends. I decided to leave school and get a job to save money. I saw an ad for Trans World Airlines (TWA) hostesses. My heart lit up. Maybe I could travel, make money, and go to school. I wasn't sure it was a great plan, but I was determined to avoid poverty and welfare. I applied, interviewed, and got hired. Off to Kansas City I went for six weeks of training. I graduated and was assigned to New York.

NEW YORK AND SHINING

I moved to New York in 1968. It was a time for deep reflection about who I was and what it meant to be Black in America. The cries for change began to permeate every medium.

Musicians were calling us out about our unconscious ways of being. Marvin Gaye; Crosby, Stills, Nash & Young; John Lennon; Bob Marley; Bob Dylan; and Richie Havens all asked us to look at how we identified ourselves and how our behavior mirrored our consciousness. Black poets began to speak out in powerful ways about politics and the state of the union. Poets like Langston Hughes, Amiri Baraka, Elaine Brown, Gil Scott-Heron, and the Last Poets leapt out with fierce and revolutionary words. I didn't understand it all, but I was still considered a Black girl with an attitude because I was a strong personality.

John Carlos and Tommie Smith were Olympians and had won gold and bronze, respectively, in the two-hundred-meter sprint. They raised black-gloved fists during the medal ceremony at the 1968 Olympic Games in Mexico City, and this became one of the most iconic sports images of the twentieth century.

The anti-war movement emerged as the Black Power movement emphasized racial pride, economic empowerment, and the creation of political and cultural institutions for Black people in the United States. The Black Panther Party moved forward. It was influenced by philosophies such as Pan-Africanism, Black nationalism, and socialism, as well as contemporary events such as the Cuban Revolution and the decolonization of Africa. Many of my friends were afraid of Black Panther members because of their violent tendencies, and white people viewed us with wary eyes.

It was also a time when women in sitcoms were making statements of independence. Mary Tyler Moore, Isabel Sanford, Betty White, Sally Struthers, Marla Gibbs, Bea Arthur, and Penny Marshall all had something to say and invited us to bring our creative voices to the forefront.

I arrived in New York as a wide-eyed nineteen-year-old. I moved into the East Side on Sixty-Third Street with three other airline hostesses. We were never there at the same time, so it was perfect. I felt so free, excited, and ready to explore. I was naive to the ways of the world, and it is a wonder the city didn't swallow me up. We partied hard. When we flew to new cities, we barely slept. Back in New York, we dressed up and went to upscale parties with athletes, celebrities, and players.

I drank martinis with an olive, and wine. I smoked cigarettes with a holder, and I felt very sophisticated. I tried marijuana, and at first it was fun. Someone tried to get me into cocaine, and that was a disaster. When I tried to snort it, I blew out instead of inhaling and blew it across the table. It is a wonder the person didn't slap me. Then I tried to eat it. I didn't like the taste and hated the way it made me feel, thank God. I dabbled in a few other drugs, but my body rejected them, and my intuition knew this was not a good path for me.

I also looked like a model, and clothes looked great on me. Men worked hard for my attention, and I felt very glamorous. I wasn't promiscuous, but I also was not really discerning. I hooked up with some dishonest playboys who had no intention of being in a long-term relationship. I spent time in some seedy bars. There is not a doubt that I had guardian angels looking over me. One man I dated was a teacher during the day and into drug deals at night. However, he really cared for me and didn't try to get me into the drug scene. He liked having me on his arm and told everyone in his world to stay away from me.

I could fly for free and share passes with my family. It was great to have my brother come to New York and to take my mom to Europe. I felt strong and successful. I started wearing an Afro while working as a flight atten-dant. This caused a stir. As I mentioned earlier, Black hair in its natural state made some Caucasians uncom-fortable. Flight attendants had an image, and Afros were controversial for many. Black people thought I was too light to be radical, and for many white people, I was a girl with an attitude making a statement. For me, I just liked the look and felt pretty. I also didn't want people telling me what to do with my hair. White flight attendants did whatever they wanted as long as they looked professional. I made sure that I looked great and that my hair was cut and looked like a hairstyle. I knew I was pushing the envelope, and I'm sure some of that feeling came from my junior high pool experience.

In my first two years in New York, I met my friend Vivian, who was an amazing singer. She lived in the fast lane and took a liking to me. She taught me how to dress and how to make better choices when it came to men. I remember her saying, "Honey, you gotta get better at your man thang." She took me to Harlem, and we hung out until all hours. We went to a club and heard an up-and-coming band called the Commodores. I really wanted to connect with Lionel Richie, but he was not interested. He was surrounded by women. We had no idea that they would become so famous.

Vivian also took me to the Apollo Theater to hear great music. The one thing she would not do was invite me to the parties at her house. She would always say, "This is not a place for you." I didn't question her. She was very clear that I didn't belong in that part of her life. I surmised much later that it was probably about heavy drugs and maybe even orgies.

I would go to Vivian's club dates and was in awe. She sang with such ease and control. I wanted to be her, but I was afraid to even mention it. I pushed down the feelings. I couldn't see a way that I would ever be as good as Vivian. I also wanted to keep her as a friend and didn't want there to be any feelings of competition with her.

Insecurity can mask itself in many ways. It can make you pull back your energy with very rational reasoning, *or* it can push you to do everything possible to get noticed. Neither works. You either swallow feelings and desires or become an annoying person that pushes people and opportunities away. It is important to become aware of passions within yourself and learn how to channel them.

I rose quickly in TWA and became an in-flight supervisor, mostly because a woman named Elaine Posta saw me. She ran the beauty section for the company and was a big fan. She convinced leadership that I was powerful and a restless soul. If they didn't give me more to do, I would be off on some other adventure. I had already begun to wear an Afro, and it shook things up. Somehow Elaine convinced them that I would be good at the job. I learned quickly and was great at customer service, and the flight crews liked me.

My history seemed irrelevant. My creativity was flourishing. I had pushed down my need to perform, but I created in different ways. The way I looked, the way I handled passengers, and the way I expressed myself seemed to be a magnet for a fabulous adventure. I had no idea what was to come, and it didn't matter. I was having the time of my life. In that moment, I felt beautiful, smart, and destined for a great life.

The '70s were going to bring some rude awakenings, but for now, the crisis of my childhood seemed far in the distance. Even the moments of conflict felt small compared to the craziness of my early years. On some level, I could sense that my past had prepared me for my present.

Challenge can be a great opportunity to move in a new direction, heal, or simply make another choice. I believe any form of crisis offers us a way to make lemonade out of lemons. This time in my life opened the portals to the liberation of my soul and yet-to-be-discovered destiny.

▶ *Exercise for the reader:*

Take some time to explore how challenge has changed you. Remember, there is an ebb and flow. Sometimes you feel like you are on a high, and other times you feel doomed. It is all part of the journey of life, and out of any challenge something new can be birthed.

I encourage you to take some time and write about your experiences. What was a moment in your life, environment, or family that became a turning point? What was happening? Who was involved? How did you feel? What decisions did you make? Were your choices supportive or destructive? You can use *one situation* or just allow yourself to remember the times when challenge pushed you into other ways of being. How did creativity come in? Did you learn to write? Did music become a refuge? Did you paint? Did you change your look?

You can see in my writing that music and clothes showed my inner artist trying to come to service. My inner artist won't look like yours, but I am clear that within each of us, a creative spark exists.

Take a deep dive here, and really look at this pivotal time. Choice point moments are always portals for transformation, even if they don't look or feel like it at the time.

We will use this information later to support bringing your voice forward and into form.

CHAPTER 4

Becoming Visible

THE '70s

- The popular band the Beatles announces they have disbanded.
- NASA's Apollo 13 moon mission returns to Earth successfully, abandoning its mission to the moon after experiencing oxygen tank problems and an explosion.
- The first jumbo jet, the Boeing 747, makes its debut commercial flight from New York to London.
- Computer floppy disks are introduced.
- In the Kent State shootings, students are killed during anti-war demonstrations.
- The US voting age is lowered from twenty-one to eighteen years old when the Twenty-Sixth Amendment is ratified.
- The Walt Disney World Resort opens in Orlando, Florida.
- The first US cable subscription service, HBO, is introduced.
- Pocket calculators are introduced.

- Billie Jean King beats Bobby Riggs in the Battle of the Sexes tennis match.
- US president Richard Nixon resigns.
- The Vietnam War ends.
- Bill Gates and Paul Allen create Microsoft.
- *Saturday Night Live* airs for the first time.
- Arthur Ashe becomes the first Black man to win Wimbledon.
- Steve Jobs and Steve Wozniak create the Apple computer company.
- NASA introduces the first space shuttle, the *Enterprise*.
- Jimmy Carter defeats Republican incumbent Gerald Ford to win the US presidential race.
- *The Muppet Show* premiers.
- The Three Mile Island nuclear incident occurs in Pennsylvania.
- The Chicago Seven are accused of conspiring to incite a riot at the 1968 Democratic National Convention in Chicago. In November of 1972, all of the convictions are overturned by an appeals court on the grounds of judicial bias and bias in jury selection.
- Michael Jackson's debut solo album, *Off the Wall*, is released.
- Iran takes American hostages in Tehran.
- Margaret Thatcher becomes the first woman prime minister of Great Britain.

The 1970s exhibited change in a myriad of ways. It was famous for fashion changes. Bell-bottoms, platform shoes, and disco made their debuts. It was also an era of economic struggle, cultural change, and technological innovation. Culture was bringing its voice out in all sorts of ways.

Many people and groups in the '70s found their way into boldly speaking up and out for justice and peace. It was not an easy place to stand. Social and progressive values that began in the 1960s continued to grow. There was increasing political and economic awareness. Liberty for women became a focus.

In 1972, after years of campaigning by feminists, Congress approved the Equal Rights Amendment (ERA) to the Constitution, which reads: "Equality of rights under the law shall not be denied or abridged by the United States or by any state on account of sex." It seemed that the amendment would pass easily. Twenty-two of the necessary thirty-eight states ratified it right away, and the remaining states seemed close behind. However, the ERA alarmed many conservative activists, who feared that it would undermine traditional gender roles. These activists mobilized against the amendment and managed to defeat it in certain places for a while. In 1977 Indiana became the thirty-fifth—and last—state to ratify the ERA.

Women were still disenfranchised and under the rule of men. But it was a time to listen to women's voices. In 1975 Ntozake Shange unveiled *For Colored Girls Who Have Considered Suicide/ When the Rainbow Is Enuf.* This theater piece told the story of so many Black women and called for us to be more visible.

Tie-dyed shirts, Mexican peasant blouses, folk-embroidered Hungarian blouses, ponchos, capes, and military surplus clothing were popular. Other attire for women included bell-bottoms, gauchos, frayed jeans, midi skirts, and ankle-length maxi dresses. Platform shoes were creating a stir. It's a wonder we didn't all break our ankles trying to be cute and stylish.

This was a time when many people became visible and allowed themselves to think, be, and say whatever they felt to be in integrity with their souls. Young people wanted to be seen and heard. They were not taking no for an answer.

Many people struggle with being seen, even though at the center of their being they long to be acknowledged, heard, and understood. Some equate visibility with physical pain. Others are afraid that being visible will bring attacks on their beliefs. The fear of losing stops people from bringing their authenticity into jobs and relationships. This is especially true within social media platforms. Today, trolls are notorious for creating vitriolic confrontations online, making people more afraid to be seen.

It takes great courage to become visible. It really means standing up for what you believe or desire, with unwavering trust that you deserve to be seen and heard.

I was becoming bolder. My dress changed and became more creative and flamboyant. As an in-flight supervisor, I got to fly to Europe and felt so important. I met famous people in many ways. I connected with the singer Rick James in a New York airport just before his first hit record. He loved that I had an Afro and a prominent position. I also partied with the Temptations in England. The world seemed so full of promise and possibility. I was living the life some people only dreamed about.

At home, my mother had found a Big Brother for David. Tom really understood him and showed him how to be in a relationship with a man of authenticity.

Right around the time I met Olympian John Carlos, I became aware of the Black Power movement. When I spoke with him, he was clear that "we as a people" had to find our voices and demand recognition for our contributions in this country and around the world. I wasn't sure I was brave enough, but his passion and courage inspired me.

I loved seeing Black poets and singers invite culture into the conversation of equality. I didn't want to be an activist, but I really enjoyed learning about the history of my people. It was amazing to me that I previously had so little knowledge of this. It hadn't really dawned on me how much being Black in America had impacted me.

One day I was walking through the airport in Los Angeles, and two men came up to me. They identified themselves as FBI, showed me credentials, and asked to see my ID. I was floored, but it didn't seem like the time to argue. They questioned me intently as they looked at my ID. Finally, one said, "Sorry, Miss. You looked like Angela Davis, and we want to talk to her."

I thought, *What the hell? Just because I have an Afro doesn't mean I am Angela Davis. Plus, how stupid do you think she is? Do you think Angela Davis is going to walk through LAX for all to see, without any disguise? At a minimum, she knows she is wanted for questioning.* I was insulted and angry, but I kept my mouth shut. I could feel the weight of my people on my shoulders in that moment. I also knew I did not have the inner courage to be outspoken about being Black in America. I was way too scared and ill-informed.

That restless spirit that Elaine Posta had recognized was taking hold. My mother was having eye surgery and asked that I come home in support. There was a chance that she would end up blind after the surgery.

I had pretty good seniority and scheduled my time off about two months in advance. I was to finish my shift and then fly to Minneapolis. When I landed in New York, I got a call saying that my leave had been cancelled and I was to fly to Washington, DC, and then to Germany. Someone had gotten ill, and they needed me to take the new flight. I was floored. I called the office and explained that I had to be with my mom and had scheduled this well in advance. I was told that I had to take this flight, period. I refused and got on the plane to Minneapolis. The surgery went well, and she retained her eyesight. I returned to New York certain that I was in big trouble. I was also aware that this was the first time that my security was not the most important thing. I'd stood up for what was important to me.

When I returned, I was called into the manager's office. I was told that my behavior was unacceptable and that I was being put on probation. The only reason I wasn't being fired was that they "understood" it was a family need. I was also told that if I was insubordinate again, I would be terminated. I sat there, and something in me shut down. They didn't care about my family need—they didn't want me making waves, bringing my problem to Black organizations, or maybe even filing a lawsuit. I wouldn't have done any of those things, but they didn't know that. I am sure my silence was unnerving. Inside of me, I seethed. If I couldn't show up for myself or my family after I had followed all the rules, this was not the place for me.

There are signature moments in a person's life, times that ask us who we really are and what we really want. Some of us become rebellious, and some of us run, blowing up our lives. It really doesn't matter how you responded. What is important is that these moments are extraordinarily significant. They can be a catalyst for the discovery of an inner knowing that wants to be recognized. To ignore or run from one of these pivotal experiences creates blocks in our growth and expansion.

A man named James O. Plinton Jr., one of the first Blacks to be named an executive in the airline industry, noticed me. It wasn't hard. There were not many Black women flying. He had been at Tuskegee Institute in Alabama and joined the flight-training staff of the US Army Air Corps as one of the first Black flight instructors of the 99th Pursuit Squadron. He was a changemaker. He told me that he saw something in me, and I was invited to join his team and teach travel to African American women. I jumped at the opportunity and left my in-flight supervisor position.

I created a fashion show with the clothes of women of color from around the world. I collected fabrics from different countries and had outfits made that could fit different sizes of women. I then went and spoke to women's organizations, had them model the clothes, and gave tips on travel, packing, and powerful destinations. I also went into the Black community and talked to young Black girls about stepping into their power. It was a dream job but came to an end abruptly and without communication. I questioned if I had done something wrong but didn't get any straight answers.

In retrospect, it was a message that it was time to go in another direction. However, that wasn't clear, and I was beginning to feel sorry for myself.

Change offers messages for growth. Most of us don't like change because it feels like we are out of control. These are moments of shift that swiftly move us into unknown territory. Since our culture does not teach us how to navigate these waters, we struggle. It is easy during these moments to make up stories and feel disconnected or even depressed. It can also create situations in which we react out of fear.

My friend Angel and her husband Bill were so loving with me. I called them my adopted family. They tried to support my erratic behavior, but I was clearly on a journey that I had to take alone. I left the airline and got a job selling media. I hated it. I was smart and could do it, but I felt stagnant. My boss told me this was going to be a powerful pathway to success, but I was bored out of my mind. I started looking for something else to do. I landed a job in an urban-development organization in Harlem. I could benefit my people and learn new things.

The creative juices were flowing within me, but I felt as though my life-force energy was draining. I started feeling lost. So what did I do? I had an affair with my boss. He was a very smart and extremely handsome Black man. He was also married. It was fun for a while, and then I discovered he was also sleeping with another employee. When I found out, I was hurt. I was still so naive about how the world worked. It didn't dawn on me that if he was having an affair with me, he was probably doing it in other places.

I was beginning to dive into a pile of depression. Alcohol and even the smallest number of drugs exacerbated my emotions. My body didn't do well with drugs or alcohol, making bad matters worse. I was also having powerful dreams about my future and people in my life. Some were prophetic (just like the women in my family had experienced for generations), and I didn't know what to do with them. I had learned early that sharing this kind of information scared people. I knew I had to take care of myself and pay rent. I looked for another job. Pretty quickly, I landed a position as an administrative assistant for *Sesame Street*. I thought it might be a way back into allowing my creativity to shine. However, the week before I was to start, I had a meltdown. I couldn't stop crying. I knew I was in trouble and decided to go back home. Even though I felt like I was returning as a failure, I knew I was headed for disaster if I stayed in New York.

What I didn't know was that my soul wanted my creative expression to come back to the forefront in a different way. I needed to go back to my beginnings, call forth my inner artist, and connect with my spiritual nature. When I got home, reentry was a challenge. My mother and brother were not getting along well. My mother had moved in with my grandmother, and they had a combative relationship. None of us were great at communication, so there were many troubled moments. I just wanted peace.

I decided to try modeling since I had done it in high school. I found a photographer and took photos for my portfolio. At the end of our shoot, he suggested I send some of my photos to the Miss Minnesota Universe contest. I fell down laughing. Who was he kidding? There was no way Minnesota was going to have a Black queen. He challenged me: "What if you are wrong? What have you got to lose?" What was this white guy thinking? I stared at him. It felt like he was offering me a challenge, so I sent in my application with one of the photos.

To my surprise, I got a call to come in and interview. I was arrogant and fully believed there was no way for me to be in this contest. I went in and was totally myself. I sat before five people and answered questions. The next week, I got a call telling me I was in the contest. I was so sure it meant nothing that I didn't tell anyone but my mother, grandmother, and brother. My grandmother made me a dress for the event, and my hairdresser did my hair. I was wearing it straight. I had let go of the Afro so that I could get modeling jobs. White people offered the jobs, and they liked straight hair.

The day of the contest, I was not nervous. From my perspective, I was in this to get noticed and get some modeling jobs. When they named the top five, I was called and smiled inside. *Nice job, Cyndi,* I thought. They asked us each a question and named the runners-up and the new queen. They named numbers five, four, and three. I was amazed that there were two of us standing there. I felt proud that I was going to be number two. Then they named the queen. "Our new Miss Minnesota Universe 1973 is Ms. Cyndi James!"

Oh my God! I saw my mother and grandmother scream and jump up. It took a moment to sink in. Wow!

I was going to New York to compete for Miss USA. Oh my goodness, it was getting real. Maybe being visible was not so bad.

Now here is the rub—I knew nothing about competing. I knew nothing about the way to dress or the politics involved in this type of competition. The people running the contest were as shocked as I was and did nothing to support my getting ready. A Black girl representing the state was not welcomed. They also did not set up any parades or events for me to show up as the new queen. I should have known that I was in for a big letdown, but I was clueless.

It was a big deal being the first Black queen in this state, and I was so excited. A shop gave me a dress to wear for the rehearsal, and my grandmother made me a gown for the actual competition. Looking back, it was all wrong. The dress did not look like a dress a beauty queen would wear. It was light blue with sequins, and the problem was that it looked like a princess dress and not a formfitting competition gown.

Off I went to New York. Miss USA didn't have a talent portion, but you had to wear a swimsuit and a gown, dance, and get interviewed. Nerves kicked in, but I was excited to return to New York a winner. At one of our events, Ed Sullivan came to meet us. He was taking pictures with us and made it quite clear he did not want to stand next to me or the other Black girl, who was from Michigan. I brushed it off because I was there in the competition. He wasn't voting, and I had more polish than most of the girls.

The entire week was filled with dance rehearsals, press events, and support on how to compete. Dress rehearsal day came, and they called out random names of final contestants just for the sake of rehearsing. They called my name, and I saw the looks on the faces of the crew. Somehow they knew the names called in rehearsal would not be the finalists. My heart sank, but I kept a smile on my face.

That night, I went to the head chaperone and told her the situation felt weird. The girl from Illinois, Amanda Jones, was acting very confident and cocky. The woman told me it was my imagination and that I had as good a chance as anyone else to win. I had made it this far, and I was a beautiful girl. She told me I should go to bed and rest to get ready for the big day. How ridiculous that it didn't dawn on me that her job was to protect the organization.

I did what she said . . . and I didn't get picked in the top group of contestants. Neither did the other Black girl. The final winner was—big surprise—the girl from Illinois. I fell apart. I went home and was basically snubbed as the queen. Not one event was scheduled. Rage flooded my being. I cried and cried. When the Black newspaper interviewed me, I told them the truth—that this state and this country were not ready for a Black queen.

My mother and grandmother told me to get over it, get closer to Jesus, and find a nice man to marry and have a family. I tried to be obedient. I went to church consistently. I even dated a couple of men. One turned out to be gay, and the other was a traveling preacher/con man. Ugh. I was sinking deeper into hopelessness.

There is no getting around the ups and downs of life. Disappointments happen. Challenges will come up. But being willing to be visible allows us the opportunity to shine the light within us. That willingness forces us to step up and step out. We are all winners, despite the outcome of any situation. Every experience prepares us for the fulfillment of the purpose that lives within us.

I stayed depressed until a man named Johnny Ricco heard me sing and asked me to join a traveling band. At first I said no. He asked, "What do you have to lose? You're not happy here. You'll be making money and be with a great band. Plus, there will be another girl from Washington, DC."

He was right; I had nothing to lose. My family was pressuring me to get married and have a family. I didn't want to do that. My relationships were not going well. Plus, I didn't know what I truly wanted. I knew I loved performing, so off I went with the group, Yesterday, Today, and Tomorrow, featuring Johnny Ricco.

ON THE ROAD

Johnny was a real character and probably a con artist. According to him, he had made and lost millions of dollars in his life. Whatever the truth, he did what he said and got us gigs around the country. We traveled in a bus and stayed in motels. We made money, but I'm not sure we got paid what we were worth. Johnny handled all the finances. The band was fabulous and audiences loved us. We played a lot of hit songs from bands such as the Doobie Brothers, Parliament-Funkadelic, Chicago, Simon & Garfunkel, and Sly and the Family Stone. Two women lead singers and one male lead checked all the boxes of a great group. The members did smoke a lot of marijuana but still played great. They thought I was a prude. One night they told me I would sing better if I smoked. I had forgotten New York and how drugs didn't really work for me. I smoked a joint and went onstage. It was a disaster. I couldn't remember lyrics or the show order, messed up dance steps, and laughed for no reason. The band tried to cover for me, but there was no mistaking I was high. Plus, all I could think about was food. After the show, Johnny told me, "Lay off the drugs." I couldn't have agreed more. It was clear that I was totally disconnected doing drugs.

The lead singer, Doug Lund, was interesting. He had one of the most amazing voices I had ever heard, and he could sing anything. He was a white boy with soul. Doug's family owned a farm, and he wanted nothing to do with farming. He wanted to be an entertainer, so this group was in pursuit of his dreams. I loved singing with him and the group, and we became great friends. Over time a relationship developed. I felt safe with him, we had a lot in common, and we loved each other.

About six months into traveling, he asked me to marry him. I thought, *This is the best of both worlds. My family will be happy, and I will get to remain an entertainer.* It was dawning on me that I belonged on the stage.

Doug took me home to the farm to meet his family. They were very nice to me, but I was definitely not into farming. I didn't want to get up before the sun rose. I sucked at milking cows, and farm chores made my body ache. I wanted to look like I was a helper, but every fabric of my being wanted to escape. As soon as we left, I made it clear to Doug that we would visit the farm once, maybe twice a year. He told me he understood that this was not a life that would support me, him, or us.

The ceremony was sweet and my family pitched in. Doug's family came and we all got along. It was fascinating how many egos in my family came forward wanting to be the leader. My mother, aunts, and grandmother vied for attention. It was astounding that the bride's desires were irrelevant. I let them fight among themselves and manage everything. We were both ready to get back on the road and get away from family, so we didn't really have a honeymoon. We immediately returned to the group and our travel schedule.

Then things started to unravel. The band started fighting among themselves. Johnny was acting weird, and the other woman singer wanted to go back home. Finally, in Las Vegas, everything fell apart.

Doug and I were clueless about what to do next. Then we heard about Jon and Helene Gregory. Jon Gregory spent most of his entertainment career on the fringe. His work in the entertainment industry included a stint with the legendary Errol Flynn, who took him to England in the mid-1950s to assist him while he made two films. In the late 1960s, Gregory ran the dance department for 20th Century Fox in Hollywood. He was also an acting coach for Jayne Mansfield, Tuesday Weld, and Lloyd Bridges, among others. In the 1970s he opened and ran the Jon Gregory Talent Center in Las Vegas with his wife, Helene. Doug and I stumbled into the studio to have a conversation. Jon worked with the singers and actors, and Helene worked with the dancers. They liked us and told us they could help us move to the next level. We decided to stay in Vegas and give it a try.

We went to classes five days a week. I worked as a cocktail waitress, and Doug did odd jobs. We got a small apartment near the Strip and only worked and went to school. It was fun and it was hard. The Gregorys were used to the studio system and pushed every student. You showed up, worked hard, and then came back the next day to do it again. All our money went to school, rent, and food.

After eight months, we both wondered if we had made a mistake, because there was no work in sight. Then, there was an audition at Caesars Palace for singers. We jumped at the opportunity. I knew Doug would get a job, but I wasn't sure about me.

We got there, and we both got up and sang our numbers. I was proud of us, but then something crazy happened. They thanked Doug and told him there was no place for him. One of them turned to me and asked, "Do you dance?"

I said yes, hoping no one would ask how much experience I had.

They smiled. Someone said, "Go to the MGM Grand hotel, and ask for Fluff. They are looking for dancers that can sing." Staff would call and tell them I was coming. I could see Doug's disappointment but had no idea the impact it was really having. It just felt like one of us getting a break was good news.

I went to the MGM and Fluff greeted me. She was a no-nonsense woman. She asked me to pirouette and then asked if I could do a grand jeté. I had just learned it and was pretty good.

When I said yes, she said, "Do some across the stage." I was obedient and did several grand jeté jumps across the huge stage.

When I walked back to her, she told me that there was a line of Black dancers, and she would like to hire me for the group. She also told me I looked like one of the leads, Patrice Chanel, and they needed a stand-in for her. They would see how it went, and maybe I could fill that role. She asked if I could start right away. Was she kidding? I was going to be a showgirl on the Vegas strip and could stop waiting tables.

I was thrilled and tried to play it cool as I said yes. She told me to stay, go into the light booth, and watch the show so I could get a feel. I would then come back the next day to rehearse. I called Doug and told him the news.

I floated up to the light booth, and my mind was blown. The orchestra started and the lights went on. Out of the ceiling came a round disc that held six beautiful Black women with lion feather hats that looked like a lions mane. They were the MGM lions. The set moved slowly to the ground for the start of the show. One number after the next came on, all spectacular. There were two amazing Black dancers, Allen and Winston (similar to the famous Nicholas Brothers); Siegfried and Roy and their large cats; and a huge water tank containing a woman swimming with a dolphin, along with a pirate ship sinking in front of our eyes. The Black girls always came in ensemble, and they were striking. I was amazed.

Fluff sat next to me, taking notes. Later, I learned that she gave notes after each performance. Her job was to manage the show and make sure excellence was maintained. I was scared and elated at the same time. I felt ready. I had really worked hard with Jon and Helene and knew I could still take classes.

I went to work the next day and stayed there for more than two years. I got to be Patrice's understudy and learned how to work on a big stage. There were fun moments as well as challenging moments.

One day I was getting ready to go onstage wearing a *Rio Rita* costume and a huge hat. I was standing by the curtain, which began to rise. The curtain hooked my hat and lifted me off the ground. I was terrified but couldn't scream. Not only was the audience going to see me dangling, but I could really be hurt. Somehow a stagehand grabbed me and unhooked the hat just before the second curtain opened. I pulled myself together and got through the number but was exhausted. Other women dancers comforted me and said this was just something that would be in my treasure chest of stories. They were right. I had a lot of crazy experiences, as did many others. The life of a showgirl was never dull. I often wondered how many crazy things the audience saw.

My mother was proud, but my grandmother not so much. She was appalled that her granddaughter was dancing with her butt hanging out. The G-string made her crazy. I told her it was normal and that we didn't dance topless. She didn't care. As far as she was concerned, Christian girls didn't show so much skin. Plus, I was a married woman. She didn't know that the marriage was struggling. Doug was facing challenges. He couldn't get a job singing and was starting to act strangely. I discovered that he was gambling our money. I asked him to stop. He said he would, but he wouldn't or couldn't—I'm not sure which. Finally, he said he was going home, and there was no way I was going with him. He left.

I bought a big, cheap Chrysler and moved into an apartment on my own. The car was a gas-guzzler, but I liked the fact that it had four doors and that the back doors opened a different way. I was mobile when I wanted to be, and I didn't have to drive much. I was aware of how Vegas pulled people down emotional rabbit holes. Dancers gambled their money away, people got into dysfunctional relationships, and it was hard to create lasting friendships. To keep myself busy, I joined a Bible study between shows and learned how to sell Mary Kay cosmetics on the side. The Bible studies were nice, but something in me was beginning to question the dogma of religion. I didn't realize that this was the beginning of a journey of spiritual awakening.

The woman that was my sponsor in Mary Kay turned out to be a godsend. I was horrible at selling Mary Kay for several reasons, the biggest being that I lacked confidence.

One day she said, "Go over to that mirror, and tell yourself you are beautiful."

I balked. "No way," I said.

She looked at me and very clearly stated, "If you don't believe you're beautiful inside and out, why should people believe you when you tell them to honor their beauty?"

I couldn't answer. She then instructed me to dress like a beautiful woman every day and look in the mirror and acknowledge how fabulous I was. It took a while, but it started me on the path of understanding that my thoughts and beliefs mattered. My inside had to mirror my exterior.

Life is all about choices, and there are no bad ones. Every single decision is a step closer to your destiny unfolding. The choices do not have to make sense or be in sync with what other people think you should do. The journey of life is not a straight line. The important thing is to know that every aspect of life is about learning who you are and who you have come here to be.

I tried dating, and the men were drunks (similar to my dad), serial womanizers, or gamblers. They did not want me to be so flamboyant and interested in sex. I was even told I was oversexed. They wanted to control the relationships. I wondered if I was ever meant to have a good or healthy love. I was lonely but had no idea what to do with myself. It was in that moment that I began to pray. I asked God to move me, to show me where I was to be and what I was to do. I loved being visible and entertaining. But I also knew that there was something else for me to do besides eight shows a week with six to eight costume changes a night, doing everything possible to avoid a note from Fluff. This was a time of discovery. I was becoming aware that I was on this earth to be seen and shine. The confusion came when people around me didn't support it.

There is something exciting and scary about being visible. Visibility is not just about being seen visually. It is about being seen inside and out. It is about learning to love yourself, honoring your gifts, and sharing them. Visibility is moving beyond fear and allowing yourself to activate the courage needed to be fully alive.

We live in a culture that does not necessarily invite bold voices. In fact, many people are afraid to say what they really think or show up in ways that might cause them to be scrutinized. They would rather do anything than be criticized or punished for what they believe, who they love, or how they behave. Here's the deal—people's opinions belong to them. You do not have to take them on.

My question to you is, what if your authentic self was just exactly what was needed to make this world a better place?

▶ *Exercise for the reader:*

How do you feel about being visible? Is it easy for you to stand out, or do you find ways to dim your light, hide your essence, and withhold your thoughts, needs, or desires?

This exercise is to get you in touch with your "visibility quotient." We want to explore where you are and the possibilities for shining your light in new and more powerful ways.

Take a few moments and answer the following questions:

1. Was I encouraged as a child to be creative and stand out? If not, what kind of messaging did I receive?
2. In which moments of my life did I stand out authentically? How did it feel?
3. What are you doing right now to become more visible?

We are now beginning to build an awareness of what might be needed for you to uncover your true and authentic voice.

CHAPTER 5

Manifesting Vision

THE '80s
- The United States boycotts the 1980 Olympics in Moscow.
- The cable network Music Television (MTV) is launched.
- The AIDS virus is identified in the United States by scientists.
- Ronald Reagan is elected president.
- Sandra Day O'Connor is nominated as the first female Supreme Court justice by President Reagan.
- Japan sells the first CD players.
- Sally Ride is the first American woman in space.
- Motorola introduces the first mobile phones to the United States.
- Microsoft releases Word, their word processing program.
- The first version of Microsoft Windows is released.

- The Chernobyl nuclear reactor explodes in the USSR.
- The Space Shuttle *Challenger* disaster takes place when the shuttle disintegrates after being launched, killing all on board.
- The Fox television network begins operations.
- George H. W. Bush is elected as the US president after defeating Michael Dukakis.
- The Berlin Wall is torn down at the end of the Cold War.
- CNN begins broadcasting.
- The Central Park Five case is in the news.

During the 1980s, conservative politics and Reaganomics were strong, the Berlin Wall crumbled, new computer technologies emerged, and blockbuster movies and MTV reshaped pop culture.

The populist conservative movement known as the New Right was growing. It appealed to different groups of Americans, including evangelical Christians, anti-tax crusaders, advocates of deregulation and smaller markets, advocates of a more powerful American presence abroad, disaffected white liberals, and defenders of an unrestricted free market. Every group had a vision and strong beliefs about how things should be.

Dreams become reality when the vision is so strong that the dreamer moves into the unknown with motivated action, unwavering faith, and a willingness to go forward in the face of disappointments, challenges, naysayers, and nonbelievers. Visionaries stay the course of their soul's desire. They will not be moved. They are the ones who show us the way, reminding us that they are examples, not exceptions.

To be a visionary is to allow the imagination to connect with your passion and allow the universe to step in to support the manifestation. It also means being willing to move into the unknown and dare to risk manifesting the vision.

Sometimes visions take a long time to come to fruition. My vision had started when I was eight years old. I had activated my imagination by creating a joyous fantasy life where I sang, danced, traveled, and expressed freedom.

I was clear that I didn't want to be stuck in Vegas but had no idea what to do next. I had trained with Jon and Helene and felt confident with my singing, acting, and dancing. I also felt comfortable on stages large or small. I got a message that there were going to be auditions for The Wiz traveling company in Los Angeles. I took time off, drove to Los Angeles, and went to the audition. The room was filled with people of every size and shape. I had never done an open call, and it was a little intimidating. I had to wait my turn and go in to sing for what amounted to less than two minutes. All they wanted was for me to sing eight bars of a song, so I had better knock it out of the park. If they liked me, they would ask me to stay. If not, it was thank you and goodbye. I got asked to stay for one round and then was cut.

I was disappointed but proud that I had tried something new. I saw a man across the room, and my heart skipped a beat. He was a tall, good-looking Black man. My friend John, who had told me about the audition, was talking to the man and beckoned me over. I tried to be cool, but I was smitten. Evidently, so was he. His name was Nate Reese, and we had one of those love-at-first-sight moments. I had forgotten the outcome of my last love-at-first-sight experience.

The rest is a blur. I went back to Vegas, and we talked for hours every day on the phone. This went on for weeks. Finally, I quit the show, packed my car, drove to LA, married Nate, and began a new chapter. It didn't dawn on me that I was moving too fast, and this was a pattern of not getting to know men in my life before I dove in. I also didn't think about what Vivian had said to me in New York about getting my act together with men. All I knew was that this man made my heart sing.

Nate was practicing the Bahá'í Faith. Bahá'í followers believe that God periodically reveals his will through divine messengers. The messenger's purpose is to transform the character of humankind and to develop, within those who respond, moral and spiritual qualities. I was clear I wasn't going to enter his faith. We agreed to support each other's faiths, even though mine was a little shaky at that moment, because I wasn't sure what I believed.

Nate was a great singer. Seeing a pattern here? He had a great baritone voice and tons of charisma. We decided to create a show together and be the Black Fred Astaire and Ginger Rogers. We auditioned for Princess Cruises and got hired to do shows for them. It was fabulous. We did our shows while traveling to Mexico, Alaska, and Australia. They paid us in cash, which really helped, and we had a great time. When we were on shore leave, we auditioned for plays, agents, and small roles. I loved Nate's family, and they loved me. Life was incredibly good.

While on one of the ships, Nate closed down. He didn't want to come out of our room unless performing. He developed a rash that couldn't be explained, and his mood swings were startling. I couldn't get him to talk about what was happening, and he kept pushing me further and further away. When we got home, he was angry, threatening, and volatile. I didn't want the marriage to end, but I became scared of him. I started planning my exit strategy. My mother and grandmother had always told me to have a bank account my significant other didn't know about. Ultimately, that advice allowed me to leave and start over. I got a job with a record producer and moved out.

Let me say here that it was not lost on me that this was my second failed marriage. It was also not lost on me that my choice of men with emotional issues was part of my pattern and a reflection of something unresolved within me.

The interesting thing about life is that it often takes several similar experiences for us to wake up. It is often said that we repeat the class, or the same experiences, until we learn the lesson. I do not believe in failure. *I believe that obstacles occur to invite us into a deeper understanding of our true calling and purpose.* Every choice creates the opportunity to look at who we say we are versus how we are showing up. If you are experiencing painful circumstances more than once, it is a call to pause and look at how you are choosing to interact in life.

After I left the marriage and got settled, I asked the cruise line to hire me as a solo act. The cruise lines were now creating shows, and I was a perfect fit. I would do my solo act and then work as characters in their shows. It was fun, challenging, and paid my bills. I did side gigs assisting the music producer so I could stay connected to the industry. I had a brief affair with the producer, dated some, and found myself in more crazy relationships. I didn't understand that I continued to choose the familiar in relationships. The men were unavailable on one or more levels, and addictions were a part of every one of them. Addiction to alcohol, drugs, women, or themselves was a glaring reality—take your pick. Some managed to be addicted to all these things at the same time.

I was depressed again and felt disconnected. My brother had come to live with me. I really love him and wanted us to be closer. However, I was too messed up to truly honor him or our relationship. I was an emotional wreck. David finally moved back home to be with his girlfriend. I was left feeling guilty and inadequate.

One day I was yelling at God. "Why aren't you helping me? If you are real, why don't you show up?"

At that moment, the phone rang. The timing was scary; I hoped I hadn't pissed off God with my attitude. When I answered the phone, it was a singer acquaintance. She asked how I was, and I decided to tell the truth. "Not good."

There was a brief silence. "Are your curtains closed? Is your room dark?"

How did she know that? "Yes," I responded.

Another brief silence. Then she said, "You're a child of an alcoholic, right?"

Warily, I said, "Yes."

"Why don't you come to an Al-Anon meeting with me? It has really helped me get through my childhood trauma with drunks."

I don't know why, but I agreed. This began a journey of unexpected spiritual awakening. I attended meetings weekly and got a sponsor. It was a multilevel experience. I felt seen by others and at the same time was afraid to share my inner world. I was experiencing a lot of shame, but I was unwilling to continue to walk down my current life path.

Desires, wants, and prayers get answered in powerful and sometimes extraordinary ways. My begging for support from God and screaming my disappointment was an invitation for the universe to step in. *The interesting thing about asking for change is that it does not always come in the way we want.* It can come as an unexpected invitation, a call, a chance meeting, an email, or a conversation. The real opportunity is to listen and trust the guidance. Where you can become stuck, and stay for a while, is when you move into the intellectual and question the guidance. It takes courage to move out of unsupportive patterns, but the payoff can be a brand-new way of being.

I decided to put my attention on acting. I took a few classes at a community college, primarily because it fit my budget. I went on auditions, mostly for independent films or plays. At first, it didn't go so well. I wasn't getting hired. I got a job at Denny's at night as a cashier and hostess, so I'd be free for auditions in the daytime. I worked from 11:00 p.m. to 7:00 a.m. and was mostly exhausted. I also was hired for a Van de Kamp's cookies campaign. They hired singers and dancers to dress up like cookies and sing outside of stores to get people interested in their products. I was a "shortbread." It was

73

silly and a little embarrassing. However, I got paid, and it was okay until I would bump into someone I knew. I would simply say, "This is what I do for love!"

Finally, I joined the Stella Adler Studio of Acting. She was a legendary coach and teacher of great actors. I got an agent and started going on real industry auditions. The roles were small—one or two days and only a few lines. One of those jobs was an under-five-line player on *Days of Our Lives*. I was a nurse named Sally Johnson. All of this was enough to get me into the Screen Actors Guild. I could finally see my dreams coming into form.

Around the same time, a woman in my life commented on how down I seemed. She wondered what my spiritual path was and thought I might enjoy a New Thought church called Guidance. I was getting better in Al-Anon, but my moods were still up and down. I didn't know what New Thought was, but I was willing to check out other ways of spiritual support, so I went to Guidance. It was in the Black community, and I was elated to walk into a group of Black people. On the stage, there was a short Black minister, Dr. Daniel Morgan. He was amazing. He was speaking without notes and was brilliant. He said, "You are the captain of your ship. You get to create your destiny. Change your thinking, and change your life."

I didn't know if I believed him, but it sounded good, so I went back the next week. I became a member, took classes, learned about affirmations and possibility thinking, and worked with teens. There was no way for me to know how life-changing that decision would be.

One of the practitioners, also known as spiritual counselors, was a man named Michael Beckwith. Today, he is the founding minister and spiritual director of a mega New Thought community called the Agape International Spiritual Center in Los Angeles. At that time, he was a spiritual practitioner and an important guide to support me taking a deeper dive into my spiritual unfolding. He taught classes at the church, hosted workshops in his home, and held weekend spiritual retreats to support awakening. It was like food for my soul. I was beginning to get bigger parts that could support me without secondary jobs. I started to see the correlation between positive mindset and manifestation.

Spiritual growth is evolutionary. It does not happen overnight. When growth operates on the physical and spiritual planes, life-changing experiences can occur. They feed off each other. The vision begins to take form through focused implementation. Manifestation occurs as mindset, intentionality, and faith intersect. The hard part is keeping your eye on the prize and having what you do harmonize with your inner work.

In the early '80s, a miracle occurred. There was an open call by Dick Clark Productions. They were looking for four girls to become a girl band and travel the country, and they would be filmed for a television show. It was the first "reality show" experiment. I showed up and stood in line with hundreds of girls. Cameras were filming the process. If they liked your look, you were invited to sing eight bars of any song you wanted, a cappella. If they liked you, you were invited back the next day to sing more. I got invited back. I had been journaling my desire to be "discovered," and this felt right.

I showed up the next day to see forty or fifty girls. I was so excited. We all sang and then waited to be told if we were going forward to be interviewed at Dick Clark's offices. I got called. Oh my God—I floated out of there. I could feel that this was possibly my big break. The only thing I was nervous about was my age. I looked young, but I was in my thirties, and most of the girls were a lot younger.

I made sure I looked great for the interview. I meditated and prayed before I went. I wanted to show up as my best self. I walked into the office and sat down before the director, Bill Dunn, and a few other people. They asked me questions. I was calm, because I remembered how it worked when I had competed in Miss Minnesota Universe. They asked me my age. I started to lie but then said, "I was afraid you would ask me that."

They laughed.

"I'm thirty-three, and I really hope that is not a point against me."

They laughed again. The director said, "Can you step out for a moment into the hallway?"

I smiled and got up. I think I was only out there for five minutes, but it seemed like a lifetime. They called me back in, and Bill said, "We would like you to come for the final callbacks. There will be twelve of you, and we will select the four from that group."

I tried to remain calm, but I am sure that my enthusiasm leapt into the space. "Thank you so much," was all I could say. I walked out, and a woman handed me music and a time to show up for the finals. I danced all the way to my car.

The day of the finals arrived. I was a little nervous. I didn't read music, but I had worked hard on all the parts of the songs and felt ready. They asked four of us to get up and sing. Then they mixed and matched us. This went on for a couple of hours. The team left the room for quite a while, and the cameras followed them.

When they returned, I was nervous. There was another Black girl there, Tyra. She was beautiful and a wonderful performer. I believed they would only pick one of us. They named three white girls, and my heart was pounding. Bill looked at the rest of us and said, "We couldn't make up our minds, so the group will now be five. Cyndi and Tyra—you are in."

We jumped up and down, hugged, and cried. We were going to be in a movie that would air on NBC, we would travel around the country, and we would sing on *The Tonight Show* the night the movie aired. Oh, and we would get paid. I knew I had arrived. Rehearsals started the next week. Candi Milo, Hillary Turk, Cyndi James-Reese, Tyra Ferrell, and Debra Rogers were on their way.

Bliss didn't last too long. Having a camera on you twenty-four hours a day is hard. Every flaw, every challenge, and every conversation is caught on film. We worked hard in rehearsals. There was no real lead singer. We all had solos. This created some anxiety in the group because some of the girls thought they should be the focus, which led to some interesting manipulation and behind-the-scenes maneuvering. Luckily, I was old enough to understand that the cream always rises to the top. The public would decide who the standouts were.

One of the girls got into a relationship with a band member, so we got to add relationship drama to the mix. It was exhausting. We played in small places, medium-sized bars, and hotels. We visited our hometowns and had interactions with family members. I honestly felt that some of the situations we were put in were manipulated by the director to create dramatic effects. Still, we were becoming a group. By the time we returned to Los Angeles, the group had started to become cohesive. We had to wait for the movie to be edited, and I was nervous. There were some moments I was not proud of because I had overreacted to some experience or interaction. Still, this was a great opportunity.

The group got media coverage; I even got a spot all by myself on CNN. We got offers for a record deal. Egos flared, and I could see that we were never going to move to the next level. People wanted to get their own lawyers and made special demands. I was a little amused. Our movie had not yet aired, and we had no real credibility at that moment. No one really knew who we were, so fighting for large contracts made no sense to me.

Reaching for the Stars was the name of the movie, and the day it aired, June 26, 1985, was exciting. We had all gone shopping for cool outfits, had our hair and makeup done, and were ready for *The Tonight Show*. Then we saw the movie. There were some wonderful moments, but a lot of it was confusing and disjointed. We were all clear that we might not get great reviews. Still, it was wonderful to see ourselves on television and then sing on *The Tonight Show*. The reviews of the movie were mixed, with the best one coming from the *New York Times*: "Overall, though, *Reaching for the Stars* offers a refreshing break in the summer season of reruns. NBC has even concocted an additional gimmick for the presentation. The Girls Rock Club can be seen later this evening as the group makes a guest appearance on *The Tonight Show Starring Johnny Carson*. The marketing continues with undiminished vigor. Break a leg."

With the band going nowhere, I got intentional about my next steps. I got television roles, took a lot of classes, did a lot of plays, and continued my spiritual studies. I had a great agent and was booking quite a few gigs. It felt great, and I could see my momentum. I was also really steeped in meditating and yoga to keep me grounded.

Make no mistake—when one door closes, another opens. The important thing is to be ready to step through the open door. That is why classes, workshops, and working with a therapist or coach is imperative. *Your preparation allows you to embrace the gifts that are being brought to you.* Nelson Mandela is a perfect example. He was preparing for leadership during his twenty-seven years in prison. He focused on his spiritual practice and anchoring his inner strength. That is why he could emerge as president of a nation. *You have everything within you necessary to succeed.* Putting your full attention on balancing the internal and the external is what creates desired results.

I was aware of what was happening in the news but was not really engaged. Looking back, it felt like my focus was mostly on my personal growth. I did love that a woman was on the Supreme Court. I also joined people on the beach for the Harmonic Convergence, the name given to the world's first synchronized global peace meditation, which occurred on August 16–17, 1987. I celebrated with a friend when the Berlin Wall fell in November of 1989 and people in that country got more freedom. Many had held that vision for years.

I was still taking acting classes, and after one of our showcases, a woman approached me. She was very complimentary and said she wanted to submit me for a show called *Star Search*. I told her I knew about the show. It was a competition, and I had sent in a tape but had not gotten a response. She smiled and said, "It's really who you know in this business. Let me submit you." I agreed, and two weeks later I was a contestant on the show in the acting category for *Star Search* 1986.

The scenes for acting were short and not very substantive. I had to come with my A game to win. There were celebrity judges every week, and I had to get the most votes to move on. With each win, the contestant received $2,000. The goal was to win $100,000. I won seven weeks in a row, which automatically put me in the semifinals—that was the good news. The interesting news was that the woman who beat me was the girl-next-door television ideal. She was perky, cute, blonde, sexy enough to garner attention, and charming.

I breezed through the semifinals, and the finals were one week away. I was thrilled to be there but was going up against the same girl who had beaten me and ended my winning streak. I got an acting coach and worked hard on my scene. I was to be a librarian who had to contend with a male stripper in the library. I was comfortable with comedy, so this felt good.

The day of the show, I had completed my rehearsal, and the producer came and sat down next to me. This was unusual. He hardly ever spoke to me. He asked, "How do you feel?"

I told him I felt good. Then he said, "Why do you think you won all those times?" It seemed like an odd question, but I said, "I'm a good actress, and I work hard." He nodded. "Yes, that's true, but I believe you really won because you brought your authentic self into the scenes. I didn't see her today." I was stunned. He got up and said, "Think about it."

My mind went crazy. Was he trying to sabotage me? Or was he giving me real support? I went to my dressing room and cried. My roommate, Peggy Blu, was competing in the singing category, and she asked if we could pray. She was also having a hard time. We intuitively knew that centering was the best thing we could do in this moment, so we did it. I prayed to be authentic, centered, and unmistakably the best. She also prayed to be the best she could be.

I went onto the stage and became the librarian. There was a line that was a challenge, and when the man took off his clothes, I flubbed the line and used the discomfort of seeing a half-naked man to get through the scene. I wasn't sure if I would win, but I felt that I sincerely had shown up as my authentic self. The nine judges, all big in the entertainment industry, held my fate in their hands: Ken Kragen, John Crosby, Cicely Tyson, Dick Clark, Bob Marcucci, Juice Newton, Alan

Carr, Lynn Stalmaster, and Michael Peters. As I walked up for the announcement, I was calm. Ed McMahon announced our names and said, "And the winner in the acting category is Cyndi James-Reese."

I almost jumped out of my skin. Joy flooded my entire being. I could see my mother and grandmother cheering in the audience. I was so glad I had flown them in. If you want to see the finals, here is the link: www.youtube.com/watch?v=AhboaUR4sFw.

The next day, my phone rang off the hook. I had written a check to myself from God and put it on my bathroom wall. The check was for $100,000 and had been there for two years. I had learned to vision cast in my classes at Guidance. I looked at that check every day. The friends that had laughed at me and my check were now vowing to write themselves checks for big amounts to fulfill their dreams. I just wish I had written a check for $10 million like Jim Carrey had. He carried his check in his pocket for years until he got a movie deal for that amount.

My mother and grandmother were so proud, and we celebrated for two days. To my surprise, once they left, I became depressed. It made no sense. I had been handed a check on national television. What could possibly be wrong? I called my friend Michael Beckwith, now a minister, to talk about these feelings. He very calmly said, "It is hard for you to be in the present. You are always looking for what's next to prove yourself."

I listened. He said, "Hang up, and walk around the house saying, 'I am enough.' When you feel clear, call me back."

I thought it would be easy, but three hours later, I was still sobbing every time I said, "I am enough." I didn't believe it, and I certainly didn't think winning this money was going to make me enough. It was in that moment that I vowed to do healing work around my self-worth. The vision of being a visible entertainer had not included me awakening my essence. Now the work began.

Just because you manifest a dream doesn't mean you have arrived. If there is self-doubt, lack of confidence, or unhealed wounds, they will emerge at some point in time. Oftentimes, it is during what seems like success. This is good news. It means that you are ready to face any inner demons that continue to sabotage your freedom. The idea is to get to the core beliefs that hold you hostage—for example, "I am not enough," I am worthless," and "I am unlovable."

I wanted to make sure I correctly handled the money I had won. My family was terrible with money, and I didn't want to follow their path. I went to my business manager, Fred Moultrie. I had hired him when I got the part in *Reaching for the Stars*. I am not sure why he took me on—he usually supported big names in the industry. I was grateful to be a client, and he helped me buy a duplex. I lived upstairs and rented out the downstairs apartment. I had made enough money to qualify for a loan and have a mortgage. I was so proud that I was becoming a grown-up. I moved my mother and grandmother to Los Angeles to live with me. They were aging, and I wanted them to be out of the cold weather of Minneapolis. I wanted them to be close so I could take care of them.

The next couple of years were fantastic. I was called by my agent to take a part on Days of Our Lives. Evidently, Sally Johnson had made an impression. I didn't even have to audition. A new character, Lexie, was being brought in to be a love interest for Abe Carver, played by James Reynolds. I didn't have a contract, but that allowed me to work one to three days a week and book other jobs. I was booking television shows and small parts in movies. My credits grew, and the '80s proved to be hot for my brand. I had guest roles on Knight Rider; The Return of Marcus Welby, MD; Trapper John, MD; Webster; Vice Squad; Magnum, PI; A Different World; Hart to Hart; and MacGyver. I even got a bigger agent.

A very well-known manager was introduced to me. Hilly Elkins handled big stars like Steve McQueen, Robert Culp, James Coburn, and Sammy Davis Jr. He thought I really had a shot. I signed with him, and he helped me get in front of some important people. Secretly, I was hoping that he wouldn't discover that I was an imposter and drop me. One day he called and said, "Lou Gossett is a client and would like to meet you."

I laughed because I thought he was kidding. He wasn't. I was invited to a hotel gathering to meet Lou. We had a nice connection, and he invited me to come to Georgia with him. I declined. I was clear that I was no star groupie. I told him to call me when he got back. The next day, beautiful flowers arrived at my home with a note saying he would see me soon.

Two weeks later, I got a call from Hilly. He told me

Lou wanted me to be his date at an event. I knew that he was a star and an Oscar winner, but I wasn't going to date by proxy. I told Hilly to tell Lou to ask me himself. A few minutes later, Lou called and invited me to a dinner. I agreed. He then told me that it was formal and I should wear a gown.

A few days later, a chocolate-brown limousine pulled up in front of my house. People in my neighborhood were hanging out of the windows and standing on their porches. Lou came to the door, told me I looked pretty, and we got in the limo. I felt like a star. Anita Baker's music played while we drove, and we talked very easily. When we got to our location, my mouth flew open. This "dinner" was a red-carpet event. Paparazzi were everywhere. I froze. Lou could see my face and put his arm around me. "Just stay close to me, smile, and I'll do the talking," he said. I slowly got out of the car, and the cameras went crazy.

We walked down the red carpet, and the photographers yelled, "Lou, over here! Look this way, Lou, right here!" I was amazed at how calm Lou was with all of this. One person yelled, "Lou, who's your date?"

He smiled and said, "Cyndi James-Reese. She won *Star Search*." I smiled, and the cameras flashed.

When we got inside, I saw Michael Jackson, Elizabeth Taylor, and more stars than I could count. I was totally intimidated. When we sat down, I said, "You saw me on *Star Search*?"

He said, "Yep—I rooted for you."

I don't remember eating. I was so starstruck that all I could do was take in every moment. I wasn't sure we would have another date, but this had made my year.

We did have another date. In fact, we got very close. He invited me to his home in Malibu to meet his son, Satie, and foster son, Sharron. We went to events, and it seemed like we had always been together. He told me he had been challenged with drugs but was now clean. Several months in, he invited me to go on a celebrity cruise with him and the kids. That made it clear we were really a couple, because this would be very public.

We got on the ship, and it was wonderful to be treated with such care. Celebrities want for nothing. The downside was the people. We were in the public eye, and every time we stepped out of our room, people wanted to connect. I understood that about cruise life, but this was another level. One day I was exhausted from smiling, talking, and engaging. The people wanting to be close annoyed me. When we got back to our cabin, Lou said, "Listen to me. Those people are why we're here. They're the reason we're public figures. You must honor them, always be respectful, and give thanks that they love you."

That was a big aha moment. It was clear I was only thinking about my feelings and not about the responsibility it took to be in the limelight. I apologized and said I would do better. That night, he asked me to marry him and gave me a beautiful ring. Our dinner table toasted and celebrated with us.

There are obligations that go with any success. To be a true winner is about understanding that accomplishment carries with it great responsibility. You are called to give and receive.

You are called to honor every aspect of the journey and give thanks for each moment. *The gift of success is enjoying the ride.* You don't have to be a public figure, but being present and kind supports any successful person. Standing in excellence on every level will deliver powerful expansion.

We got home, and shortly after, Lou had a relapse. Cocaine was the drug of choice, and Lou would disappear for a day or two. Our lives were thrown into chaos. The enabler in me wanted to protect him and keep the kids safe. I did all the things you are not supposed to do to deal with an addict. I joined Hilly in making excuses, hiding things, and manipulating schedules. That went on for months until I got tired. I told him I couldn't do it any longer and moved back to my duplex. I don't know if it was me or the challenges with his career that moved him into rehab. I think it was a combination.

While in rebab, we had couples' sessions and family meetings, and he had group sessions. I was not a big drinker, but I was aware that my personality changed slightly when I drank. My dad's alcoholism could be hereditary. When Lou announced there could be no liquor in the house, it was easy for me to stop drinking. I could see familial patterns were playing out in my life and reflected in my relationships. I had dated several men with addictive behaviors. Quitting drinking seemed to be in alignment with that knowledge and understanding of my spiritual nature. Plus, I felt and looked better when I was not drinking.

Lou was ready to get married, but I wasn't. I wanted to see if the sobriety lasted. He stayed sober, did family things with me and the kids, went to meetings, and stayed close to home. I moved back in, and we began to plan the wedding. He was doing another *Iron Eagle* movie that was to shoot in Israel. We decided to get married there. It would be small. The only people who would attend would be the kids, my mother and grandmother, and a few people from his staff and crew. We would take a honeymoon after he completed shooting.

I had a gown made by an unknown Black designer, and off we went to Israel. My mother was so happy to be the mother of the bride that she smiled the entire time. My grandmother was an avid reader of the Bible and had wanted to go to the Holy Land her entire life. This trip was a gift that lifted her spirit into a space of bliss. We had a driver and bodyguards that made it easy to sightsee and feel safe.

We got married in a hotel in Haifa, by a Baptist minister no less. I am not even sure how we found him or even got permission to have a ceremony. The kids put up with our joyous vibes, but clearly they would have been happy to stay home. The only big deal for them was when Sharron got to ride a camel. He loved it.

It was during this time that I realized that my childhood dreams had come true. I was an actress and a singer. I was married to the man of my dreams, living an abundant life, traveling around the world, and recognized as a public figure. I had no way of knowing that in the next decade, my life would take some drastic turns.

I believe we are all visionaries. Our dreams are signals from our soul that we are here by design. An important thing to remember is that there is no destination. The journey is the gift, no matter how long it takes. No matter how many obstacles, the adventure is the prize. We are here to express fully, be fulfilled, and shine the light that is our essence. Many people have lost the vision because of life circumstances. That does not mean the vision is dead; it is just dormant, *and* we have the capacity within us to awaken that energy and bring it into form.

▶ *Exercise for the reader:*

This is an exercise to tap into the visionary that lives within you. You may not remember all your dreams as a kid, but you have certainly had dreams as you have grown. Do some stream of consciousness writing. Write down every dream or desire you can remember ever having. They can seem silly or seemingly frivolous. Just write. You might have wanted to be a doctor, police officer, dress designer, world traveler, painter, singer, parent, spouse, dancer, island dweller, or news anchor.

Once you finish writing, circle the ones that you have experienced on any level, large or small. The circled ones are the signals from the universe that you can design your life. You can look at past vision boards or journals if you have any doubts about what has occurred.

Don't judge those things that didn't work out or places you may have stalled. You only want to focus on what you have accomplished. Everything that has happened to you is a part of manifesting the vision and destiny of your life.

Keep this list; we will use it as we continue.

CHAPTER 6

Silent No More

THE '90s

- Tim Berners-Lee publishes a formal proposal for the World Wide Web.
- East and West Germany are reunited after the collapse of the Soviet Union.
- The Internet becomes available for unrestricted commercial use.
- The lead singer of the band Queen, Freddie Mercury, dies from AIDS.
- Democrat Bill Clinton is elected as the US president.
- The Mall of America opens in Minnesota.
- The North American Free Trade Agreement (NAFTA) is signed into law.
- Nelson Mandela becomes president of South Africa after being elected in the country's first multiracial elections.
- The online-auction website eBay is founded.

- Princess Diana and Prince Charles get divorced. She dies in 1997.
- In twelve months, Internet host computers go from one million to ten million.
- The search engine Google is founded.
- Apple reveals the iMac computer.
- President Bill Clinton faces impeachment proceedings.
- The Y2K problem, also known as the Millennium bug, is the most important thing on most companies' minds in 1999. There was a possibility that critical industries such as electricity or finance, and government functions, might stop working at 12:00 a.m. on January 1, 2000. This fear was fueled by the press coverage and other media speculation, as well as corporate and government reports. All over the world, companies and organizations checked and upgraded their computer systems.

The '90s became the highway for human interconnectivity. The Internet brought new ways of getting information and sharing facts, statistics, and knowledge in an instant, and it would not be silenced.

It felt like a time of extremes and contradictions. It was also an entire decade of relative peace and prosperity. A gallon of gas in 1990 was $1.34! A new house could cost $123,000, and the average cost of a new car was $16,000. Americans were building bigger and more elaborate homes and driving more expensive automobiles. It was a time of working harder to pay for the debt that was being accrued. I was certainly in that category. I spent more, borrowed more, and went more deeply into debt. Talk about trying to keep up with the Joneses.

Musical movements emerged such as grunge, rave, and

hip-hop. They spread around the world to young people, supported by new technologies such as cable television and the World Wide Web. It was as if the entire world wanted a voice; they needed to be heard and expressed. At the very same time, I was opening to something new within me. My inner warrior was being born.

I was soaring in the early '90s. It was as if I had a gold spoon in my mouth. It didn't dawn on me that my mother had shopped for comfort, and I was doing the same. Actually, living above my means.

I was amazed that the Soviet Union fell, ending the decades-long Cold War and scary messaging. The rise of the Internet and technology alarmed me. I didn't think my brain could move fast enough to comprehend what was happening. The level of communication expectations was taking a quantum leap, and I felt stupid and ill equipped.

The role of Lexie had come to an end. They wouldn't offer me a contract and wanted me to turn down other roles to be on call. My agent and I refused. I was booking almost every audition I went on, including television, movies, and plays. It was impressive that I was on shows like *The Nanny*, *True Colors*, *The New Lassie*, and *227*. I was also booked in the movie *Ghost Dad* starring Bill Cosby and directed by Sidney Poitier. Lou got a lead role in a movie called *Diggstown* with James Woods, Bruce Dern, Oliver Platt, and Heather Graham. They called and offered me the role of Lou's wife. I was thrilled. When they edited it, they cut down most of the female roles. It was disappointing, but the movie was still a credit on my résumé.

Our marriage hit a wall when I talked about having a child and Lou balked. I felt like the time was now or never. Before we married, we had agreed to have at least one more child. When he pushed back, I asked to go to therapy. This proved to be a huge awakening, and it was not about having a baby. Our therapist was a recovering alcoholic. Lou felt comfortable with her, and I liked her a lot. In our sessions, we would start to move, and then it would come to a screeching halt. I blamed Lou, and of course he blamed me. One day I was angry at the direction the session was going. The therapist looked at me and said, "Did your father hurt you?"

At that moment, something blew up in me. I fell on the floor, curled up in a ball, and sobbed uncontrollably. Lou was stunned and couldn't move. The therapist got on the floor with me and slowly helped me get back in my body. I had disassociated (emotionally left my physical body because the pain was too intense). Memories that made no sense came flooding in. It was clear I was traumatized. She suggested I get a personal therapist to explore childhood trauma, and she would continue to work with Lou and me. I did just that. I found Dave Grill. He specialized in connecting with emotional wounds and body reconnection.

Many people are on the fence about therapy. There are all sorts of perceptions and misconceptions about what it means to get therapeutic help. My family didn't want to "let other people into our business." Others are so entangled in shame syndrome that opening to vulnerable experiences creates fear responses. Here's the thing—*healing requires support*. It might not be a traditional therapist, but I believe we all need someone in our lives that can help us move beyond limited beliefs and patterns. Someone that can guide us to a deeper understanding of our choices, inner contradictions, and fear-based behaviors. What is important is not to rely on someone that does not have the consciousness to help you move to another level of awareness. People that will cosign unsupportive beliefs only assist us in staying stuck.

The next few sessions with her were okay, and I was feeling better about the marriage. We were talking more and really spending family time together. I would travel with Lou to his movie sets when I wasn't working. Lou felt that we could stop our work with her and just stay present with each other. That probably wasn't the best move. In the meantime, Dave Grill was really helping me. I was getting in touch with unresolved rage. Childhood memories came to the forefront, and I was devastated that no adult had taken care of me. I was also caught in an old pattern of giving my power away.

Because Lou was an Oscar-winning actor, we got invited to many places. One of those places was the White House. I was terrified. I had no idea how to act, what to wear, and what would be expected of me. I felt pretty good about my style. Lou was a great teacher and would take me shopping for clothes that fit the image of a public figure. When the call came for the White House, Lou found a stylist to assist me in selecting clothes. But this still didn't address how to show up in a political arena. Hilly and his beloved supported me. They reminded me how to sit and, most importantly, to listen more than I talked. That helped with my insecurity. I really wanted to make a good impression for Lou and for me.

When we got to Washington, we had two big events. One was a lunch, and the other was a gala that ended at the White House. The lunch was unnerving, because Lou sat at a celebrity table, and I was at a table with politicians and a couple of military leaders. This was a moment I was happy to be pretty and to remember that men liked to talk about themselves. I asked a lot of questions, listened, and smiled. People thought I was wonderful.

At the gala, I held on to Lou's arm, smiled when introduced, and took a photo with President Bush and his wife. I don't think I ever felt comfortable or like I belonged. I did, however, make a good impression. Lou and Hilly were both proud.

During that time, I was singing on telethons with big names, and my notoriety as a singer was rising. One day I got a call from Hilly. Rich Little, the comedian and impressionist, had seen me sing on a telethon and wanted to have a conversation. We both lived in Malibu, so we had a meeting. He wondered if I would like to be his opening act at Harrah's. Holy crap!

I was blown away for two reasons. One, this was an amazing opportunity. Two, I had no show, no big-band charts, and no showstopping gowns. Of course I said yes and then worried about how I was going to pull all of this together. Lou told me to call on my music friends for assistance.

My friend Eric was brilliant. He had made a chart for me to sing in an international competition in Puerto

Rico, which I won. People loved my singing and the composition. I called Eric for support, and we went to work on a thirty-minute show. Something came alive in me, and my showgirl training allowed me to shine on a big stage.

Opening for Rich initiated a new chapter. I also got to open for Jay Leno and traveled the Harrah's circuit. I had my own dressing room and was treated like a star. Lou and some of my friends came to my shows, and I even got to perform for Sammy Davis Jr., who was opening the next day. When he showed up at my dressing room to congratulate me, I almost fainted. I felt so empowered and so proud. When I walked on those stages, I felt seen, and more importantly, heard.

Isn't it interesting how people can be living in dual realities? They can feel successful and accomplished at work yet judge their personal experiences as failures or struggles. We are in a culture that does not teach us how to navigate life's waters. The messaging is to keep your career and personal life separate. That is interesting to me, because we live in both areas of life. The challenge becomes connecting to our authenticity and bringing that into every job and relationship. Where it gets slippery is knowing how to reveal your inner power and articulate it in every situation, especially when people are used to you being one way and don't love that you are changing.

I loved being a mom. I really tried to balance my career and supporting the family. When I was home, I went to games, attended school conferences, took the kids places, and worked with our nanny to make sure the children were supported and kept busy. We had legally adopted our foster child together and made sure Sharron was in therapy to help him navigate the transition from life with a challenging birth mother in St. Louis to Malibu life. We even found ways to stay connected to his siblings. I was baffled why his mother kept having babies she couldn't care for. Sharron's older brother, Lee, would become a big part of my life.

Lou's biological son, Satie, was a challenge, because his mother hated that Lou was remarried and that she didn't have free rein to come and go as she pleased. The nanny who had helped raise him for many years was an advocate for his mother and supported her with access, food, and money. When Lou got clear about the dynamic, he let the nanny go. Satie was upset and went into therapy also. Through trial and error, we found someone to help us with the kids. We were a show business family and needed someone to assist in creating stability. There were times I felt guilty, but there was no way for me to handle all the areas of our lives alone.

I was very involved in my spiritual studies and personal therapy. I felt sure that the change in my consciousness and emotional state was directly affecting my status in show business. It felt like a great balance for the celebrity life I was leading.

One day Hilly called and said Disney was doing a new pilot with Cristina Ferrare. They were creating a different type of talk show featuring her and three other women. It was a precursor to The View. I went in for an interview, and they immediately booked me. We were going to do four weeks of the pilot. Every weekday morning at 5:00 a.m., I was on my way to the studio. We met in Cristina's room, went over notes and segments, did a little rehearsal, and went live. It was amazing. We talked about our families, our goals, and our challenges and had guests of every kind. We covered women's issues, gender issues, and funny stories about our lives.

We even did a show the morning the news broke about Magic Johnson being HIV positive. He was a friend of Lou's, and we really wanted to be conscious about how we handled the conversation. I told the story of having a conversation with the kids about safe sex. I shared that Sharron and I were very close and how one day he'd told me he knew all about condoms. I told the audience that I was shocked. I had said to him, "Tell me more."

He looked at me with so much confidence and said, "I simply put the condom on before I leave home, and then I'll be ready." The audience roared, and I got to tell them how I navigated helping him get clarity on the subject.

I was my most authentic self. I even did a demonstration on self-defense. My therapist, Dave, had supported me in taking a class where I could learn to fight for myself, since I had felt powerless as a kid. Men in huge suits would attack, and we learned how to fight and escape. Something in me was changing, and I was feeling more powerful than ever before.

Then shift hit the fan. Lou was doing a movie and was in training for the role. He stayed at a hotel in the city, and I stayed home with the kids. I was doing a photo shoot in our home when I got an urgent call from my agent, Claudia. She told me that the *Enquirer* had called and asked about Lou and I splitting up. I was stunned. We had gone through more challenging moments and even went back to therapy, but we had never talked about separating. Claudia told me Lou had filed for separation, and it was coming out in the paper.

I hung up the phone, immediately went into the bedroom, and called Lou. I asked him if this was true. All he would say is, "You should get a lawyer."

I was numb. The camera crew was in the living room, and I knew I had to complete the shoot. I got myself together, finished the day, and collapsed. I stayed in my room because I did not want the kids to see me in such despair. It was clear that I had to pause, get still, and allow myself to process before I made any moves. I told the nanny I didn't feel well. My mind was reeling. The thought of another failed marriage flooded my mind, and all I could do was cry.

No matter who you are, there are times when it feels like you have been run over, beat up, or attacked. That is not the time to be reactive or make snap decisions. Automatic responses get us into trouble and sometimes create more chaos than the original event. Challenging moments call for stepping away from the circumstances to calm down. It is a time to pause, reflect, and breathe. This could also be a time to get support from professionals and people that love you.

I didn't know how to get a lawyer or move through this. I talked to my therapist and called some friends to assist me. Meanwhile, the *Enquirer* story came out, and I had to tell the kids. I tried to be calm, but I was a mess. I interviewed several lawyers, and all they wanted to do was take Lou to the cleaners. That was not my style. I didn't even want the divorce, and I certainly didn't want to go after his money. I had married for love, not possessions. Meanwhile, Lou wanted me to move out of the house. Hilly told me Lou wouldn't divorce me if I gave up my career and traveled with him. I was livid. He'd known who I was when we got married. I was not giving up what I loved. My mother and grandmother were living in my duplex, and I didn't want to go there. Plus, my family thought Lou walked on water.

I finally got a lawyer I trusted, and he advised me not to leave our home until we had clarity on paper. Then it got ugly. I found out Lou had been seeing multiple women and was back using drugs. Some of my friends knew but had been afraid to tell me. HIV was on the rise, and I was terrified that Lou had passed something to me. He wanted custody of the kids. I had no rights to Satie, but Sharron was legally my son. I was not going to leave him in a house with a nanny while Lou fooled around, was using, worked nonstop, and was never there. I went to see Reverend Michael to ask for support. He reminded me that I was in a fight with a warrior I could not beat. Lou had the name and the resources to beat me on every level. He advised me to get clarity about what was nonnegotiable and only fight for that. I was sure that I was unwilling to give up my son. I was unwilling to sit back and allow my son to be disconnected from me. My voice was awakening.

While the lawyers fought it out, we were advised to go to a mediator. Lou said things about me that were not only untrue but also unkind. He even wrote a document that painted me as an unfit mother. I was mortified, so much so that I could not get out of bed. I was immobilized.

The lawyers hammered out an agreement, and I went to stay with my friend Shirley Jo until I could get a place. In the meantime, Lou's attorney insisted that Sharron be asked who he wanted to live with. He was twelve, and she thought the court would listen to his desire. I flipped out. Lou had all the perks, and he wouldn't be there to give guidance to a teenager. It was a kid's paradise. My attorney told me I had to go along with this plan or it would create more drama. So I agreed, and my greatest fear was realized. Sharron chose to live with his dad and Satie. I was awarded one day a week, every other weekend, and alternate holidays.

Some people in my life were upset. They thought we were the perfect couple. As I lay in bed at my girlfriend's, I felt as though my heart had been ripped out. She came in, crawled into bed with me, and stayed until I cried myself to sleep. As I was waking up, I was once again calling out to God in my mind, *Why is this happening to me?* The song "Everything Must Change" came into my head. The words kept spinning over and over:

Everything must change,
Nothing stays the same.
Everyone must change . . .
Nothing and no one goes unchanged.

Then a very small voice in my head said, "You have always recreated yourself. Now is no different. Get up and create a new life. Your son is supported." A peace came over me, and I got out of bed and got busy finding a new home. I journaled, prayed, meditated, went to therapy, and worked out.

Sometimes the most difficult, painful experiences are the catalysts for incredible change. The hard part is learning to listen to your inner knowing when it is hard to get up off the floor. That is why we all need a tool kit for overcoming chaos. That tool kit will become a place where you mine the treasures of the universe. If you can become still enough to expand your consciousness, the world will meet you right where you are and provide guidance. It is not easy, but it is worth it when you learn that no situation has the power to hijack your life. *The answers to your prayers might come in surprising ways.*

One day I was driving down the street, and billboards of Lou's new movie were everywhere. At one point, I yelled, "Why is this happening to me?"

A quiet voice in me said, "Because you are to see the God in him. He is a great teacher for you." In that moment, I knew this was a spiritual message for my expansion. I began to send blessings to Lou in my spiritual practice.

I found a home and was grateful for any time I had with Sharron. I continued to go on auditions and do gigs. A public divorce is hard, and I was challenged with staying focused. I tried to stay connected to Satie, but he was in a hard place. I had gone to therapy with him and told him how important he was to me and that I wanted to stay connected. After a while, it was clear he had to choose his father. Meanwhile, Sharron was struggling in school and even took his father's key to the BMW and tried to drive. Luckily, he didn't kill himself or anyone else. The nanny got him back home and put the keys away.

I showed up to his events and encouraged him to stay focused on his education. One day he came home with me and told me he wanted to come live with me. I was a little surprised. He told me his dad was hardly home, and when he was, he had girls over with very little clothing on. He was sure Dad was using drugs again. He didn't think it was a good place for a kid. I told him that he was going to have to tell his dad's attorney, since he had told the courts he wanted to live with his father.

To my surprise, he called Wendy, the attorney, and told her exactly what he had told me. I called my attorney and shared what was happening. I told him I was not going to try to smear Lou's name. I just wanted my son. Shortly thereafter, Sharron moved in with me, and child support was arranged. Lou and I never spoke, but I heard rumors that he had some not-so-nice things to say about me to mutual friends. Many Hollywood friends chose to step away from me. I was told by other celebrities' wives that most people choose the celebrity when separation or divorce occurs.

I drove Sharron to school, got ready for auditions, and did stuff around the house. I also watched a lot of television. It never dawned on me that I was still depressed. I would just become aware that hours had passed and I was sitting in front of the television. That was the beginning of me understanding "distraction."

The mind is amazing. It is so sophisticated and capable of moving us away from pain. The unfortunate thing is that it usually leads us to people, experiences, and dramas that move us to disconnect and discontent. I call these things "distractions." A distraction is what prevents someone from giving their full attention to something else, or it can be extreme agitation of the mind or emotions. It might be both. Either way, the outcome is doing anything and everything that moves us out of feeling. The challenge with that is there is no hiding place. Those feelings will continue to rise until you face them.

When you decide to recreate yourself, you are starting over. This is good and interesting news. The good news is that you get to move into a space of creative regeneration. Who do you want to be? What brings you joy? What depletes you? How do you want to live? What kind of relationships do you want? You get to build yourself from scratch. The interesting news is that this is an uncomfortable void, where nothing is clear.

I had a prayer posse of six women: Tina Lifford, Debbie Gayle, Rene Featherstone, Chemin Bernard, Eisha Mason, and Shirley Jo Finney. Over the years, we supported each other through many life transitions. I am not sure how I would have navigated this time without them. Shirley Jo is an amazing director. One day I told her about a dream I had. She knew I was a prophetic dreamer and said, "I think this is a one-woman show. Let me help you develop it."

I wrote, and she did the dramaturgic work. It took my mind off life challenges and allowed me to be creative. As I was writing, I was aware that my entire life had been about silencing my voice to be safe. If this play came into form, that would have to change.

I was still in therapy, and Dave was helping me see how hard my childhood had been. We uncovered the impact of the sexual abuse by my stepfather and the abandonment by my biological alcoholic father. He continued to help me diffuse the rage flooding my being. Why hadn't my mother taken care of me? Eventually, I confronted her, and she cried. She said, "You were young, and I didn't think you would remember. I had no place to go and no way to take care of us."

I was screaming. "He beat you and me! He raped me! You were supposed to take care of me!" We ended up crying, with no resolution, but I was grateful that I finally was able to express the pain I was feeling.

Sharron's older biological brother, Lee, still lived in St. Louis but would come and visit us on occasion. We loved sharing time, Disneyland, and our spiritual community with him. They had a special bond, and I loved supporting them staying in touch.

Then Lee's guardian, his grandfather, passed away. Lee tried to connect with his biological mother, who now had eight or nine children. She wanted nothing to do with him. Sharron came to me and asked if Lee could come live with us. I said no; I was having a hard time taking care of us. Sharron was a negotiator and shared how Lee had supported him when he was little and their mother was struggling. Their biological mother had left

Lee in the hospital when he was born, and he deserved a break. I was still against it but told him I would think about it.

Here is where it gets interesting. God, Spirit, and the universe would not leave me alone. In my meditations and dreams, and even while I was on walks, I was told to support Lee. I was told repeatedly that he was my child. I mean, really? Didn't I have enough on my plate? Finally, I had a call with Lee and told him that when he graduated from high school, he could come. I told him he had to be in school, because being educated was essential. He agreed. What he didn't tell me was that he had been in trouble.

One day he called and said he had completed school and was ready to come. It didn't dawn on me to check on his school records. Once he arrived, we found out he had lied about completing school. I was furious and almost sent him back but told him he had to get his GED or he couldn't stay. We found a place, and he went to school. What we discovered was that he was smart but he'd had no guidance. After he got his GED, he got a job and entered a community college.

During that time, there were men interested in me, but I was clear that I was the common denominator in all my failed relationships. If I was going to have healthy love, I had to get healthy. Therapy, spiritual classes, and my prayer posse were my anchors for months.

My acting career was in a slump. The play with Shirley Jo felt like a great way to energize my career. I took money from my savings and rented a theater on Sunset Blvd. to debut my one-woman show, *The Hand of God.* It used all my talents: dramatic acting, singing, dancing, writing, and comedy. Also, it told my story without edits. I was energetically "naked" and vulnerable in each scene. I wanted this to be a place where the industry could experience my range as an actress.

Shirley Jo was relentless. She would not let me hide. When I got scared to be revelatory, she pushed me, especially when it came to including the sexual abuse from my stepfather. She told me that I had to be real if this was going to be a success. I had to find my voice.

People seemed to love the play and wanted to ask questions, so after each performance I had a Q and A, and then I created workshops. It was the beginning of what would become my purpose revealed.

I started to get bookings in small national theaters, theater festivals, spiritual communities, and nonprofit fundraisers. It was fun, but it wasn't really creating enough financial support to sustain us. On top of that, no agents, casting directors, or managers were beating down my door. Still, I held out hope that someone would recognize my talent and make me an offer I couldn't refuse.

I also had to make some choices to take care of Lee, Sharron, and myself. I volunteered to sing and work with teens at Agape, Michael Beckwith's center. It was growing fast, and being in service was wonderful, but it was not going to create stability. I was still supporting my mother and grandmother. That had its own challenges because their relationship was complicated and often contentious.

I was praying for assistance. I didn't know what to do. My skills were in entertainment. I reached out to one of my celebrity-wife friends and told her my situation. She was so kind and told me that her husband loved me and might be able to help. What I didn't know is that her husband, Dennis Holt, was the founder of Western International, a huge media-management firm.

Dennis was known to have a kind heart, and it showed when we met. He understood how much I loved acting. He sent me to the human resources department to get a part-time job until my next big job came. I had no sense of what pay was in the corporate arena, and I asked for too high a salary. The woman smiled and offered me an hourly wage to "help me get by."

I gladly accepted, and she had me start by screening applicants. Turned out I was good at it. I kept thinking acting was going to pick back up, but it didn't. I would get callbacks, and then the job would go another way. A movie role would be between me and another woman, and she would get it. It was so frustrating. What I didn't remember was that I was asking the universe for clarity.

There is a saying: "Be careful what you ask for." The universe is powerful and will give you what you seek. If you are asking to be clear, it will show up in support of that completely. In my case, one of those moments was when I had seen Lou Gossett on a TV show at my girlfriend's house. I had said, "Let me be clear. That's what I want. He is the kind of man I want to marry." The universe heard me.

Your request may not end up looking like you think. It could reveal itself as a cheating spouse, a lying employer, an addicted friend or family member, a challenging workplace, or a crazy financial situation due to mismanagement.

What is important in these instances is to understand that the experience is an answered prayer. It is an opportunity to shift perception, make a new choice, or change directions. In my case, it turned out to be all of the above.

That job at Western turned into a seven-year transformative experience. One day I was walking down the hall and passed the office of a man, Daniel Roth, who I shared niceties with on occasion. He smiled and asked me to come in. He had been promoted and was moving across the street, next to Dennis's office. He wanted me to come and interview to be his assistant, full-time with benefits. I didn't want to give up on acting, but something told me that the interview couldn't hurt, so I went. He was going to head up an international division and thought we would make a good team. I was quiet. He sensed my reticence and said, "Think about it, and ask your heart." (This was an interesting request from a corporate executive!)

I left and walked back to my office. Every time I thought about saying no, my heart constricted. When I thought about working for him, it opened. I took the job.

Meanwhile, working with teens proved to be a big deal. One of the kids, Rosa, was struggling and almost homeless. My kids asked me to help. I wanted to say no, but once again my heart was saying yes. I told her she could live with us. I gave her ground rules and took the money from the state for her care and put it into a bank account to support her when she turned eighteen in a year.

Within weeks, she broke the rules by smoking weed and dating a married man. Sharron and Lee didn't want to snitch on her, but I soon caught on. I sat her down with the man from the state that worked with challenging teens and we gave her an ultimatum: honor the rules, or go into a shelter. She chose to honor the rules, stay in school, and get ready to be independent. She has grown into a successful woman.

A pivotal moment occurred in 1995. Lee had come to me with a proposal: he wanted me to adopt him. He was twenty years old. He had done research, found the legal documents, and thought it through. He told me I was his real mother. We got a paralegal and submitted documentation. The day of the court hearing, the judge read Lee's letter. I had not seen it. He asked Lee if he'd written the letter, and Lee said yes. The judge smiled. "Adoption granted."

We hugged, and I got to read the letter. I was so moved by how articulate he was about why he was my son. I was deeply touched. My heart flew open and has stayed that way. In that moment, I remembered that I had been told, internally, that he was my child. In that moment, there was no doubt.

Around the same time, I was asked to sing with the choir at a prison. The Agape Choir, under the direction of Rickie Byars, was amazing. It was an honor to sing with them. A few days before, I had been in the bookstore when a man walked up to me. I had just given a speech for the teens, and he complimented me on it. The funny thing was, I felt my heart "smile". I was still on a dating hiatus, so I didn't give it any thought.

The next week we were at Terminal Island prison and had to stay in the parking lot to honor extra security. We were out there for a long time, and that same man walked up to me. I was wearing an orange sweater. He said, "You look great in that light." I was annoyed. That was a stupid pickup line. I looked at him and said, "What are you, a photographer?" He smiled and said, "Yes, I am." Turns out he is a world-renowned photographer.

I felt a little sheepish but played it off. We talked for a very long time, and he asked for my number. Internally, it was an instant yes, but I didn't understand it. He wasn't my type. Plus, I was on a hiatus. Why did I want to give him my number? It made no sense, but I gave it to him. It took him two weeks to call.

In the meantime, I had a dream about being a minister. I had resisted this calling for years. I called the School of Ministry, and they didn't call me back. I thought, *Great. I knew this wasn't for me.* But then my intuition told me to check out a place called the University of Santa Monica. They had master's degree programs in spiritual psychology. It seemed perfect, as I was already a licensed spiritual practitioner and counselor. I picked up the phone and called USM. They called me back in five minutes.

Intuition is a gift, and it is not linear. It comes in many forms—dreams, hunches, downloads while journaling. However it comes, my advice is to listen, pay attention, and act. The rest will unfold in ways you never imagined. The hard part for most people is when the message comes in a way that defies the rational mind. It tells you to go left when you have been taught to go right. *Intuition is connected to a field of possibilities that does not know time and space.* It sees potential and invites us to take the journey as it supports our greater yet-to-be. Learning to trust this inner knowing and still-small voice is the task we must all learn if we are to leap into our most powerful selves.

Carl Studna did not fit my relationship vision physically. He wasn't a person of color. He wasn't an actor. He wasn't a tall, athletic type. He wasn't a hyper-charismatic man. Instead, he was a good-looking, slim, calm, spiritual Jewish man. He had been on a spiritual path since his teens and was a well-established photographer. His specialty was portraits. I had been photographed by many celebrity photographers, but when Carl took my photo, it was me. He captured my essence.

Our first date was magic. We talked for hours, sharing deep spiritual insights. I told him I wasn't looking for one-night stands or frivolous connections. What I wanted was to discover what a conscious relationship looked and felt like. I'm sure my being so direct was overwhelming for him, but he hung in there. I had my list: single, available, ready for this relationship, loves his family, loves God, sees and honors me, and loves my children. I hate to admit it, but he seemed to be all of those things and it scared me. If he was real, I was going to have to look deep within myself for how I created love challenges.

My children were not sure about him. What was I thinking, bringing this white boy home? One afternoon, Carl and I were having a disagreement in the car, and the boys came on the porch and stood there with their arms crossed until I told them everything was okay. They stayed cautious, but over time they began to see what I saw. This was a man of light and integrity.

When I shared with Reverend Michael my confusion about falling in love with this man, he said, "You either believe in God or you don't. You can't decide how love shows up."

If you are in a place of seeking love or wanting to deepen your relationship, something is essential. You must be your authentic self; dare to bring your voice, needs, and desires; and step up and trust that love will not elude you. Then, when it shows up, don't question the form. Form can change, but *love is eternal and will show up in the way you need it at any given moment.*

I started to grow locks; I wanted to be my naturally beautiful self. Carl volunteered to help me with my play. When he had time, he coordinated the music during my performances. He even came with me to do the play and a workshop at the prison for men at Terminal Island, where we had first connected. I was excited to have a partner that wanted to share in my dreams. Then, all of a sudden, he shared that he needed some space.

I was taken aback. What the hell did that mean? He shared and I listened. I told him, "You can have all the space you need. I'm out." I was done with chasing men to convince them to love me.

He was surprised, and we didn't talk for several days. He finally called and said he wanted to go to a spiritual counselor. He had been in this place before and wanted us to end consciously. I agreed.

I was deep into USM and was learning amazing tools. Thus, speaking up to Carl seemed easy. Plus, one of our assignments at school was to create our own counseling strategy. I created the tools I use and teach today. I learned to use all the practices and processes to heal myself and be authentic while I was in this program.

One night I woke up suddenly and felt like something had happened to Carl. I called the next day, and he said he was okay. However, in therapy he told me he had gone on a hike with a girl he had met at an event. He liked her. My heart felt shattered, but I didn't say anything. My agent had asked me if I thought I wanted to live my life without Carl. In that moment, I knew I didn't. But if he was dating other people, I sure wasn't going to tell him I felt this way. Eventually, Carl told me he wanted to commit. Neither of us was sure we wanted to marry because we had both experienced failed relationships. But we did want to be together.

Things were changing rapidly. My grandmother went to live with her daughter on the East Coast. My mother wanted to go back to Minnesota to be close to her brother and sister.

Sharron was in high school and struggling with his grades. He wanted to go to college. So, I enrolled him in a college prep class to support testing. I also got him a tutor to fill out applications. He was dating a girl, Shannon. I knew they were sexually active and I reminded him to be careful and cautious. This was no time for a baby in his life. He told me he was being careful.

Sharron got accepted into college, and we were both filled with glee. It was the first time I had seen him so excited and confident. Just before he was to leave, his girlfriend announced that she was pregnant. They wanted to get married and have the child. I resisted, but here we were. I contacted Lou, and we met with Sharron and his therpist, Shannon, and her mother. We encouraged them not to have this child. Sharron was not mature enough to be responsible for himself, and we didn't want him to recreate his early childhood. Lou and I agreed—a rare situation—that this was a bad idea. We were both clear that they were headed in a direction of struggle. They told us they had a "plan," but it was full of holes. I wondered why her mother was not asking more questions.

When I tried to share with my son that he was not ready to be a parent, he vehemently told me, "This is my life! You have no control." Truer words were never spoken. I realized in that moment that I had done all I could to prepare him to be an adult, and he was now choosing his path. They were married in my living room, surrounded by our spiritual community and the Christian community of his new wife. They had agreed to introduce their children to both spiritual paths, but I knew on their wedding day that this was a fantasy compromise. It became more apparent when they moved in with her mother.

Sharron went to Philadelphia to attend college. Shannon refused to go, even after Lou offered to pay for an apartment for them. She wanted to be close to her mother until the baby was born, and then she would move to Philadelphia so he could complete school. He lasted less than one year and came home to be with his wife and daughter, Brionne. Shannon was then diagnosed with lupus and clearly would not leave California.

My heart felt broken. It became clear that he had created a journey of struggle and would probably not go back to school for a long time, if ever. That turned out to be true. These naive children seemed so ill-equipped to create and manage a strong marriage. Within a short period of time, another child, Mycah, was on the way, and they were beginning to struggle.

I felt like I was on a supercharged roller coaster. Even though I was working, I was still struggling financially somewhat. I sold the house and moved back into my duplex. Lee was really upset. He loved that house and no understanding of managing life transitions. Then Western merged with Initiative Media, and I got several promotions to support departments and events. They trained me, and I learned a great deal about the new technology. I found out I wasn't stupid. In fact, I could learn quickly. I ended up in corporate communications and managed the intranet for the company.

Carl moved from his long-term cabin in Beverly Glen and in with me. We did a lot of work together and got married on August 29, 1999. We spent our honeymoon in India at a conference for the Dalai Lama, which Carl was photographing, and in Bhutan. It was clear to me that learning to speak my truth had created something powerful . . . a healthy, loving relationship.

Let me say here, *learning to speak up is not for the faint of heart.* It is uncomfortable. It can feel scary. It can bring to the surface some of our deepest fears. It can also liberate you. It can bring to your awareness how incredible it feels to be bold in every area of your life. It will also attract your heart's desires.

117

Like attracts like. If you are clear, strong, powerful, unapologetic, and daring, the universe will bring in the same. If you are not, the same universal law applies.

I am clear that Carl was a manifestation of my shift in consciousness and willingness to tell the truth and be silent no more.

▶ *Exercise for the reader:*

This exercise is twofold. Let's take a moment and reflect on where you are in the moment. Do you need to take a pause or recreate yourself? We will explore which places within you need light so that you can bring your true self to the surface.

Please take out your journal and look at your current reality. Are you in need of a shift and don't know how to get there? Are you trying to push through life, and you feel exhausted? Look at this list. Whichever ones apply to you, write them down and journal all the feelings, upsets, and confusion that may be driving you. Please don't judge. This is an exercise to open the portal of possibility.

▶ SYMPTOMS OF NEEDING A PAUSE

1. You cannot seem to shut off your mind.
2. You feel confused about the choices you need to make.
3. You do not take the time to eat properly.
4. You do not take the time to exercise.
5. You feel overwhelmed in many areas of your life.
6. You do not take the time to connect with your family.
7. You do not have a *centering* practice that supports you.

Once you are clear about what needs to be addressed, let's choose some tools to assist in freeing you so that recreating yourself will have focus and clarity.

▶ PAUSE TOOLS

1. Make yourself a priority.
2. Start your day in the quiet (minimum of *five* minutes).
3. Say *no*. It's a complete sentence.
4. Create affirmations that you say daily.
5. Engage your passion points (calendar them).
6. Commit to radical self-care.
7. Be honest with yourself.
8. Ask for help.

Recreating yourself is not easy, but it is transformative. Below are some ideas to help you move to your next level of awareness. If you are an overachiever, please know that you do not have to do all of these at once. These are just ideas to jump-start your process. Start with one, and when that feels successful, move to another.

I have used all of these tools many times over to reinvent and recreate myself.

1. **Pause and reset:** Take conscious steps to rest, sit down, look at the sunset, listen to calming music, or read a book.
2. **Reflect and refocus:** Think about, or journal, what is really important to you. What and who makes your heart smile? What lights you up? What do you love that you have put aside until you "have time" to get to it?

3. **Movement is medicine:** Do something daily to get the energy of your body moving. Go online and find yoga classes, dance classes, and stretching sessions. Lots have emerged during the pandemic.

4. **Clear and make space:** Now that you have time, what can you organize, clear, or clean out? What spaces (closets, drawers, files, and so on) need to be cleared to make room for something that could support you moving forward?

5. **Ready to receive:** This is where your powerful imagination comes in. Start visioning and visualizing new ways of being and expressing. You don't have to know how to get there. Let the dreamer inside of you go wild. Write it down.

6. **Exploration:** Start playing with ideas. How can you rejuvenate an idea that has been on hold? What classes are available online to support your ideas? Who can you collaborate with to create new ventures? How can the artist in you come alive?

7. **Get out of the box:** Try new stuff. There is nothing to stop you from experimenting. You've got time and space. Let your inner child and inner artist come out and play.

8. **Practice using your voice:** Start small. Have courageous conversations with people that you love and trust. Let them know it isn't easy but that you really want to live an authentic life and appreciate their support. This is a great exercise if you are having a disagreement. You get to practice being what you want.

We will take all the exercises you have been doing to support forward movement by the end of the book.

CHAPTER 7

Emerging

2000–2010:

- The use of mobile phones moves to an essential consumer.
- On September 11, 2001, known simply as 9/11, nineteen hijackers simultaneously take control of four US domestic commercial airliners. The hijackers crash two planes into the World Trade Center in Manhattan, New York, one into each of the two tallest towers. Within two hours, both towers collapse. The hijackers crash the third aircraft into the US Department of Defense headquarters, the Pentagon, in Arlington County, Virginia. The fourth plane crashes into a rural field in Somerset County, Pennsylvania, following passenger resistance.
- A series of anthrax attacks spreads fear among the American public.
- George W. Bush creates the Department of Homeland Security to fight threats of terrorism.
- The No Child Left Behind Act passes, and President George W. Bush signs it into law.

- An estimated forty million people are now infected with AIDS or HIV.
- The space shuttle *Columbia* disintegrates over Texas upon reentry, killing all seven astronauts on board.
- Facebook is launched as a social networking site only open to students from Harvard.
- Martha Stewart is convicted of a felony and sentenced to five months in prison.
- Hurricane Katrina strikes the Louisiana, Mississippi, and Alabama coastal areas. Levees separating Lake Pontchartrain from New Orleans, Louisiana, are breached by the surge, ultimately flooding roughly 80 percent of the city of New Orleans and killing 1,600 people.
- The video-sharing website YouTube is founded.
- Nancy Pelosi is elected as the first female Speaker of the US Congress.
- President Bush and House leaders agree to a $150 billion stimulus package, including rebates for most tax filers of up to $600 for individuals, $1,200 for couples, and an additional $300 per child for families.
- Barack Obama becomes the first African American president of the United States.
- The writers' strike against Hollywood studios, networks, and production companies demands a percentage of revenue instead of a fixed fee for Internet content. The strike lasts for one hundred days.
- After being struck by a flock of Canada geese shortly after takeoff, US Airways Flight 1549, piloted by Captain Chesley B. "Sully" Sullenberger, makes a successful crash landing in the Hudson River.

- On June 25, 2009, the death of the King of Pop, Michael Jackson (the most successful entertainer of all time), brings worldwide outpourings of grief.

Time seemed to be accelerating. The US vulnerability to terrorists became a reality. HIV and AIDS became a huge issue, and the concept of free love was challenged in a big way.

The 2000s began with a lot of discomfort, change, and refocusing. The writers' strike in Hollywood pretty much put a nail in the coffin of my work in the entertainment industry. Technology was beginning to soar, and it was clear that I had to step into a new way of being or be left behind.

During this time, I was still working for the media management company, and there were a lot of things that had changed, because they had merged with an international company. My boss, Daniel, left, and they had moved me into corporate communications. That was disappointing, because I had carved a niche for myself working with the departments my boss oversaw. I was using tools I had learned at USM and could see results in the leaders and the teams. Financial goals were met and exceeded. The teams were communicating, and it was exciting to see the growth. Just before Daniel left, he told me to keep my head down. I wasn't sure what that meant, but I soon found out.

Lee had been hired at Initiative and was doing well. He had even started dating a girl, Monique, at the company. It felt like things might be falling into place for him. We had a falling out, and he moved out and got his own place. This proved to be a gift. He realized what a responsibility it was to manage his money and needs. I was proud when he invited me to dinner to see his new place.

My new boss, Patty, was smart and likable. She saw that my event-management skills were good, and she had me continue to oversee corporate events. She even hired Carl to take executive photos around the country. During the transition before she arrived, I met with the chairman of the board and did a presentation on what I had achieved. I thought he got it, but the next day HR called and told me they wanted me to manage the intranet and all these different technical things. I freaked out. I wasn't tech savvy, but they said they would train me. The sentiment was take it or leave it, so I stayed—I had responsibilities. I struggled for quite a while, but there was a part of me that was glad to learn new skills, and corporate communications was very interesting.

Please be aware that when your life is changing, it shifts in increments that often don't make sense. Job offers that are not your passion will come. You will receive invitations to events that might not seem like your cup of tea, have visions that make no sense, or have dreams you haven't thought about for years. Pay attention—the universe is always sending messages to guide you to your next grand adventure.

We had gone through Y2K in which every company was afraid that all the systems were going to shut down. We had been doing all this work, and it turned out to be nothing. There was lots of panic, and then nothing happened when we went into 2000.

Emerging

In 2001 I woke up one morning and my phone was ringing. My girlfriend said, "Turn on the TV." It was September 11. We witnessed airplanes hitting the towers and people dying. One of the people connected to us called to say her brother worked in the Twin Towers, and she was terrified that he was dying. Many of the executives in the media management company were in New York, so I was in Los Angeles with only one other leader. Meanwhile, people were really upset. The other leader and I decided to take the conference rooms and turn them into meditation spots where people could go and just be quiet.

The company had two buildings, so we went to each building and invited people to come over, and we simply let them talk. Some people cried because they had family members that might be dead, and there was no way to know. Those meetings created a loving and wonderful connection with the staff. Because I managed the intranet, I put out an email requesting the names of staff's churches, synagogues, or whatever places they thought people might need to gather and be supported spiritually. I made a list and put it on the intranet. Three days later, the phones were back up in New York, and the Internet was working again. My boss called me. She said, "What are you thinking? We are not a spiritual organization. What are you doing putting that stuff up there and turning the conference rooms into meditation places?"

At first I was quiet, and then I don't know what happened. I said, "I'm not afraid. If we cannot take care of each other now, what's the point?"

And she said, "I'll talk to you when I get back."

I hung up and just sat there. I don't know if I was more angry or disappointed. My mind started racing. *All right—when she comes back, I'm probably fired.*

That did not happen. They had received so many compliments from staff saying, "Thank you for taking care of us," that she didn't dare fire me, but there was tension. I noticed that every time I walked in that building, I was in emotional pain and angst. At one point, I went to HR and told them I was having anxiety attacks. This was because the job wasn't in alignment with my frequency.

I want you to know that if you are doing something or in any relationship that is not in alignment with your soul call, energy, and frequency, you will be uncomfortable. You will be in pain. The mind will not be able to remove it. People are brilliant and sophisticated. They find ways to push feelings down; hide through drugs, alcohol, or sex; or just run. None of that matters. You will take the energy with you.

I was already a spiritual practitioner as a counselor. I was seeing people, and I was hoping that my work with people would amp up so that I could make enough money to walk away from the corporate job I didn't love. I wanted a soul feeding.

It was interesting that my singing had taken a turn, even though I wasn't doing theater or hotel stages, or traveling anymore. I got invitations to sing in spiritual communities. I had been a Broadway type of singer, so I had to find music that fit my voice and my style at the same time. I was able to use positive songs and lyrics in these spiritual communities. These jobs did bring me joy.

The other offers were also still connected to theater. I got invited by Deaf West to come and choreograph *Romeo and Juliet*, in which one family was deaf and the other was hearing. It was a challenge, but it was wonderful. It fed my soul too. I even learned a little sign language. It was used in the services at Agape and was headed by a talented actor, Paul Raci, who worked closely with Deaf West.

I realized that I really was burning the candle at both ends. I was trying to work this job, be a great mother, serve as a spiritual practitioner, and stay in my expressive nature. My body was saying, "You should slow down."

At the same time, Carl and I were doing well and growing. I changed my name back to Cynthia. I was no longer a Cyndi. I was completing my degree at the University of Santa Monica. When I enrolled there, I hadn't been exactly sure what I wanted to do. But during that time, my deep passion for supporting people and helping them heal, especially through trauma, was soaring. I was asked to create my own counseling strategy, and what would become Emotional Integration was born. I also created a meditation CD called *Shadows to Light* as my graduate project. It covered purpose, inner child connection, transforming of memories, and releasing rage. These were areas that I had personally worked on and had seen come up with clients and in my workshops.

I missed singing and noticed that lyrics were coming through in my journaling. Sometimes music would pop into my head, and I would record the melody or lyrics. I found an amazing pianist at Agape. Martin Lund was very talented and played many instruments. We recorded my first CD in his garage. I was in awe of how things from my journal became music I truly loved. *Standing in the Light* was my entry into the world of spiritual music. Carl shot my cover, and I felt very proud of my achievement. It was like I had been reborn through music.

I was having this kind of inner dance going on. I wanted to be more and do more but didn't know how. I would do a workshop here and there, and some people would attend. The workshops were small, and people liked the content. It seemed like a lot of work to do for an audience of six to ten people. I began using my music in the workshops and discovered the power of music to heal. I also added movement to support clearing energy in the body.

My meditations kept telling me that the content that I had written and performed for my play was about freedom, so I created a workshop on becoming free. People kept asking for it to be a book. I didn't know how to write a book, so I procrastinated and gave handouts instead. I had friends who were writers, and they kept saying, "Just take a deeper dive. Take a deeper dive." I did, and the book *What Will Set You Free* was born.

I felt so insecure. Then my old boss, Daniel, sent me this poem, and a portal in my mind opened.

Emerging

Graffiti Koan

Roaring down I-95
thirteen or fourteen summers ago
van full of boxes bags
and apprehension
new wife
my thirteen-year-old daughter
who would lose her way
due to my own neglect
start a new life
in San Francisco
speeding through the derelict streets
of Connecticut
old abandoned mills
life gone by
then I see it
across a footbridge
between the projects
shaky graffiti scrawl
not flowing tattoo-like swirls
this guy must have hung from a fence
cars flying by at seventy miles an hour
and I see his words:
What will set you free?

—DANIEL ROTH

Reprinted with permission from the author from his book
Ordinary Life: In Three Acts

129

The book was born, and I used the poem to open it. In my meditations and journaling, I kept getting the idea that I was going to have hundreds of people in this workshop. It made no sense to me, because a very small number of people always showed up.

What I want you to know is that when you have a vision—when it comes through, when it is connected to your passion—*there's no time and space in the universe.* That vision doesn't mean it's going to happen next week or next month or even next year. It means that it's percolating within you, and that you are a container for it to be birthed through. You are pregnant with possibility.

As soon as I graduated from USM, several things happened. The dreams about my being a minister came back with a vengeance. I did not want to be a minister, so I resisted. Nothing in me thought ministry would be fun. Agape invited me to support a spiritual conference, and during one of the sessions, I had a mystical experience. I kept getting the guidance to speak to a man in the room. The inner voice kept saying, "Get down on your knees and tell him." I resisted. There was no way I was doing that in a room full of people.

A talking stick was being passed around. People were to do a completion sharing, then pass the stick to the person next to them. As the stick passed, the voice got louder, and I refused. I began to cry. It was clear that I was arguing with God.

By the time the stick got to me, I surrendered. I got down on my knees in front of the man. I don't remember

Emerging

what I said, but when I stood up, I saw a vision of me in a robe on a church platform. I then heard, "This is no longer a request." When I sat back down, I realized the dean of the ministerial school was sitting next to me. In my mind I said, "Okay, I will go, but you better make this easy for me." (For those of you who haven't realized it yet, I talk to God or the universe in direct ways.) I looked at the dean and said, "I'm filling out an application for school tomorrow." The man I spoke to shared that what I told him was an answered prayer.

During this time, a lot had happened with the kids. Sharron had left his marriage and was using family members to enable his challenging behavior. Finally, we did a family intervention, and he tried to commit suicide. I felt helpless and guilty but knew we had to take drastic steps. He agreed to go into a program with the Salvation Army to get support for what was diagnosed as bipolar disorder. This was not a pleasant experience. However, while he was there, he discovered that he loved to cook. He worked in the kitchen, and when he was discharged, he enrolled in a cooking school. My heart exhaled.

Lee had dated a lot of girls and somehow ended back with Monique. They asked me to do a commitment ceremony to support their love. They were not ready for marriage but seemed determined to make the relationship work. I felt that their exposure to spiritual principles could really help them realize their dreams. Lee was also going to night school to get his BA.

I started ministerial school, and the entry process was easy. I prayed to be supported, nurtured, and held

131

while in school. I also asked for an exit strategy from my job. Seemingly out of nowhere, calls to sing in other communities, client inquiries, and invitations to teach and speak came pouring in. I was making money doing what I loved.

I got a phone call from a spiritual community in Denver, Mile Hi Church, which is one of the largest New Thought communities in the world. I had wanted to sing there for many years, but I didn't know how to get in touch with anybody that would hire me. The call was from the musical director, whose name was Kent Rautenstraus. He said, "We've heard your music, and we would like for you to come and sing at Mile Hi."

I smiled and answered, "Wow, that would be great!" We made a booking, and I got on a plane to Colorado. I took my CDs of music and meditations and my book to sell. I looked like a professional traveling artist. I even had charts for their amazing band.

What I didn't know is that Mile Hi had a female singer for quite some time who had left the community. They had hired a man to replace her. He was also an opera singer, and while I was there, he was in New York performing. I brought a different kind of energy. It was fun and a wonderful experience. I was very grateful.

A few weeks later, when I got back to Los Angeles, there was a music conference at Agape. It was led by singer and songwriter Rickie Byars Beckwith. She invited spiritual singers, musicians, and music directors from around the country. There were a lot of us there. She guided us into a meditation, and during that process, I heard within me, "You can go for a little while."

I thought, *Go where for a little while?* I opened my eyes, and I realized that sitting next to me was Kent from Mile Hi. He said, "I would love for you to come for a month to Denver and be our artist-in-residence."

I was looking at him and thinking that it was so amazing that I heard the answer to this question before he asked it. What I didn't know is that Mile Hi had never had an artist-in-residence come for a month, and he had not asked the senior minister. That idea had come to him in the meditation. I said to the universe, "If they will pay me my monthly salary for that month, then I will go. I will quit my job and trust the divine."

They offered me the exact amount of money I made per month. They would also pay for travel and an apartment. They even hired my husband to come and take photographs of the ministerial staff. I put in my resignation and committed to this new adventure. I still had one year of ministerial school left, but this felt right.

At the end of the month, we went home. My clients were doing great and referring me. I was going to school. It was wonderful. Here's the interesting thing—from the moment I said yes, my spiritual counseling practice blew up. People started coming and were happy to pay my fee. I made enough money, between going to Mile Hi and seeing clients, to pay for ministerial school and take care of all my bills.

I was living what I taught. The moment I left that corporate job, it was an exhale. My stomach stopped hurting. I slept better and was calmer. I didn't know what was going to happen next, but I knew that something powerful was occurring in my life and I could trust it.

In the fall of my final year of ministerial school, Carl and I went to a conference given by the Association for Global New Thought. We decided to go because it was in Palm Springs. While we were there, Dr. Roger Teel and Kent, the musical director, asked us to have tea. Just before our meeting, Carl said, "They're going to invite you to Mile Hi."

I said, "No, they're not." He just smiled.

When we sat down, that's exactly what happened. Dr. Roger said he would like for me to come to Denver and be an associate minister.

"No, we're not moving out of California and moving to Denver. I grew up in Minnesota. There was snow, and I'm not moving back to snow," I said.

He looked me in the eyes and said, "Well, why don't you just take it into prayer?" I hate when people tell me that, because I usually know that there's something deeper to understand. We took it into prayer, and we took it into a visioning process, asking the universe for the highest vision.

The answer kept coming back, "Go to Denver." It was scary for Carl because a lot of his business was in California. But the universe kept saying, "Go to Denver." Carl had also gone to USM, and he had graduated, so he had learned to listen to his intuitive knowing. It took me a couple of months, but I called Dr. Roger and said, "Okay. We're coming."

"Okay, I'm going to take this to the board," he said.

In January, he called me back. "We want to offer you a letter of call [which is like a contract]. And you'll come, and you'll start in August." It was a fantastic and generous offer.

It was also interesting, because Carl and I had felt for some time that we would be leaving Los Angeles. We would drive around, talk about our dreams, and look at places in California. We had done the same thing while in Denver, but not because we wanted to move there. We just wanted to open the field of possibilities. We were both clear that future casting through visions was powerful. Reverend Michael had supported me in becoming the vision-core coordinator for the larger organization, and I hosted meetings to vision for the future of the next steps for religious science. I knew the process worked.

I do want you to know that *when you start having thoughts and visions and desires, pay attention to them,* because the universe is trying to tell you that there's a calling. Something is trying to get your attention. There's something bigger and more profound that is moving you. *When you listen deeply, actively trust it, and become obedient, the universe syncs up with you in ways you could never have imagined.* Follow those instincts to explore new possibilities. Then sit back in an expectancy of good, and witness the miracles of life unfold.

It was very clear to me that this was a God call. This was a God shot. Carl and I had come to a little bit of a wall when he said, "I'm not sure I want to go."

I took a breath. "I have to go where God tells me to go." It wasn't an ultimatum, but I was clear he had to make his own choice. He chose to go. Now we were faced with the challenge of telling our family. The kids were freaked out that I was going to be leaving.

I decided to sell the duplex and that we would put our money together to buy property in Colorado. I had to finish ministerial school, graduate in June, and move. In May, Carl went to Denver to look for a house for us.

We knew that we wanted a house with property because Carl wanted to have a horse. We were looking for a place not too far from Mile Hi since I was going to have to commute. We also didn't want to be on some mountain road where it would be dangerous to drive.

We created a vision board that held all these needs. I started taking ministerial exams, and Carl called me, very excited. He was in Denver and said, "Oh my goodness, I've found our home. It's perfect. It's twelve acres." He described this place and said, "You need to get on a plane to come and see this before it's sold."

I was quiet. "I cannot get on a plane. I'm taking ministerial exams. If it's ours, it'll be ours. Tell the guy that we'll give them five thousand dollars to hold it for two weeks until I complete my exams. Then I'll come and look. But if I don't like it, he's got to give us our money back."

Carl was anxious. "He's not going to do that."

"Well, then it's not ours," I said. He reluctantly asked, and to his surprise, the man agreed.

I completed my exams, and we flew to Denver. It was summer and really warm when we landed. We drove for a long time before finally arriving. The house was at

8,700 feet, and when we got out of the car, it was cooler. I do not like to be cold. We stood on the property, and I got very emotional and scared. I said, "I don't want to walk the property. We'll come back and see it tomorrow."

We got back to the hotel, and I was anxious. It made no sense to me, but I couldn't sleep. I was up and down all night, and every time I'd try to meditate, I kept hearing, "You have to take care of the land. You have to take care of the land." I was confused. *What do I know about taking care of the land?*

I got back into bed and looked at Carl. He was also awake. I said, "I cannot take this house for you." We both cried in each other's arms when he said, "I know."

We got up and went to the house. The real estate agent was there. She had shown us around when I was the artist-in-residence. The house was totally *not* my style of decorating. It looked very mountainy. Carl shot me a look. "Don't judge it by the decorations. Feel into it."

The house had a good energy. The views were spectacular, and the sunroom sat right in front of an amazing tree. Carl and the man who owned the property were already connected and went down to the barn. The real estate agent walked me through the property, and it felt good. We walked down to meet the guys at the horse area where there were four acres of grazing land. We walked out into the meadow, and as we were standing there, it was like I was in a movie. I looked out, and I saw energy waves coming toward me. The energy moved over my head and through my body. I was tingling all over. I heard, clear as a bell, "You're home." And I started weeping.

The realtor didn't know what to do, so she hugged me. Carl and the man didn't know what had happened. I pulled myself together and said, "Okay, this is where I'm supposed to be." I realized the reason I had been scared the night before was that it was so big.

What I want you to know is that sometimes when things are so big, so powerful, and so beyond where you have been, some part of you will want to stay small. Don't allow it to win. You are here to be grand. You're here to be glorious. You're here to be powerful. You're here to stand in your greatness.

We moved to Denver, and I started at Mile Hi. It was everything I could have wanted. It used all my skills. I got to speak and support the music ministry, the women's ministry, and the LGBTQ ministry. It was so amazing. I got to teach classes and oversee the three hundred spiritual counselors of the community. Because Mile Hi is huge, it was run very well. I loved the way it was organized. Everyone had a role. The ministers met and collaborated, and the system for volunteers was extraordinary. I felt like I had been gifted. This was 2003, and I flourished and thrived over the next few years. I was learning a lot. I could see how every aspect of my life had led to this moment.

Every path you take, every experience, is part of the amazing journey called life. Nothing is wasted. The ups and downs are all part of growing into the person you came here to be. The opportunity is to remember this during great change or transition.

In 2005 I got a call from a woman who went to Mile Hi who said, "I go to Chartres, France, and there's a labyrinth there." That interested me because we had a labyrinth at Mile Hi, which we walked monthly. "They're looking for a facilitator. And I'm wondering if you would like to come."

I thought, *Well, that would be great.* "Sure. What does that entail, and how long would I have to be gone?"

She said, "I'll check. Why don't we see if anybody else wants to come with you?" To my amazement, sixty people signed up to go on this trip. We had to create two groups, thirty in each session. It didn't dawn on me to ask Roger if he felt it was okay. It would be on my time off. It also never dawned on me that none of the other ministers took people on trips—only Roger.

We went for two weeks. We spent a little time in Paris and then moved on to Chartres. Each group stayed for a week. We worked with a woman named Lauren Artress. She is *the* most renowned labyrinth expert in the world. I didn't know at the time that this was the beginning of me taking people on pilgrimages, but there was something amazing about supporting people to take inward journeys in sacred locations. Chartres is a magical place, and the cathedral has the largest indoor labyrinth in the world. People fell in love with the place and had powerful healing experiences.

The trip wasn't just for the group. I also had a mystical experience. While I was at USM, I was in a trio with a woman and one of the cocreators of the university, Mary, was doing a guided meditation. While I was in the meditation, I had a vision of this place with many women in a circle. There were stairs and a giant cauldron with fire underneath it. I saw the women being killed and me dying in that place. When I opened my eyes, the woman that was sitting in front of me, a woman that I really didn't normally relate to, said, "Did you see the women?"

I thought, *Yes*, but I didn't want to get into it because it seemed too out there. I just nodded.

Years later, I was in Chartres. It felt transcendent. Lauren got permission for us to have a private walk in the labyrinth after it closed to the public. In the bottom of the cathedral (crypt), there was an old well. There was also seating just below a Black Madonna statue. It was night, and we were sitting and doing a prayer. I was singing a song to help get ready to walk. We were then each given a piece of paper. On the front of the paper, we were to write what we were letting go of, and on the other side, what we were receiving. I was letting go of pain and wounds from the past and was receiving freedom. I walked at the front of the group with Lauren. As I walked past the well, something stopped me. It was like something was energetically pulling on me. I know it sounds weird, but I was getting a message to put my hand on the well.

When I put my hand on the well, I just sobbed. Finally, I pulled my hand away, and I thought, *I'm one of the leaders; I'm not supposed to be out here having a meltdown.* I kept walking and came to a woman holding a bowl for us to put our sheets of paper in. As I was doing so, she was looking at me, and I started sobbing again. I got to some stairs and looked up. I realized that these were the stairs that had been in the meditation at USM. I walked up the stairs, and this stillness came over me. A very small inner voice said, "You are walking the ancestors out." I later learned that this was a place where women had been tortured and thrown in the well so invaders could poison the water.

When I got to the top of the stairs and rounded the corner, I saw candles all around the labyrinth. This was the fire that I had seen in my vision. What came to me in all my journaling at the end of the night was that I had been walking those women out, as well as my own ancestors—even the women who had been abused over time. It was extraordinarily powerful. I felt like something was moving in me. I didn't know what it was, and I didn't know where it was going to take me, but I knew something was creating a shift.

You don't have to travel to a foreign country, have big visions, or have mystical experiences to change. Every person navigates his or her spirituality in his or her own way. The important thing is to stay awake and be present in your life. *The universe is constantly sending messages and signals to support your healing and transformation. There is no one way to transform.*

Lee and Monique had gotten pregnant, and she had a miscarriage. They came to be with us to grieve. We did a ritual of release and called in the child that was to come through them. This turned out to be revelatory.

Monique got pregnant again, and a few months in, we were told the baby had Down syndrome. They needed a lot of support to decide how to handle the situation. They agreed to keep the baby, and Zion, the most amazing soul, came into our lives. It was clear from the beginning that he was a bringer of light and love for the entire family.

Carl and I had made some financial agreements before we moved. He was not keeping some of them, and I was not bringing up the subject. I was avoiding it big-time and was aware that I was quietly shutting down and becoming resentful. I was also aware that I didn't want to blow up another relationship. I just pushed down the feelings and kept busy.

One day on a walk, I brought up my feelings, and we had a civil conversation. He promised to do better, but things did not change. I tried to pray, meditate, and journal, in hopes that somehow he would make a shift. When it didn't happen, I knew I could no longer spiritually bypass the subject. I invited him to dinner in a public place. It was important to not have a fierce fight. After we ordered, I told him that his not keeping the agreement was a deal breaker. If he couldn't find a way to shift, I was out of the marriage. He got angry and said I was judging him. He was right. I was judging, *and* the situation was no longer acceptable. I spoke my truth. I gave him one year to get his act together.

That was not a fun year. I couldn't talk to anyone at Mile Hi about it. I could reach out to my prayer posse, but we weren't as close as we used to be. We both got separate support and went into therapy together and had some intense sessions. I was really wondering if relationships were for me.

This was also a time when Mom was in transition.

Emerging

She had been living in an assisted-living apartment. It was wonderful. She had independence, and a staff looked in on her. One day I got a call that she was having a physical challenge and had to have surgery. I quickly got a flight to Minneapolis to be with her.

After the surgery, the doctor informed me that she could not go back to living alone. I had seven days to find her a place and get her out of her apartment. I called several places, and they had no space. Mom was a pack rat, so I had to clear out stuff and decide what items were essential. I knew she was not going to like my choices.

One night I was sitting in the middle of the floor surrounded by boxes and trash bags. I felt powerless and disheartened. I called my prayer partner, and he said something profound. "You only have to do one box at a time. You only have to make one call at a time." I took a breath, thanked him, and continued to fill one box, one trash bag, at a time.

The next day, I got a call. Mom had been going to a senior day care connected to a nursing home. The woman calling loved my mom. She said, "There is a space opening. Someone just passed away. If you want it, tell me and I will make it happen." It was a nice facility with good family reviews. I jumped at the chance. The interesting thing was this woman had been the first person I had called.

The next day, I had to tell Mom about the developments. She didn't resist, because the rehab place she was already in felt like a place people were sent to die. I told her not to worry. My brother was estranged, but my cousins would assist, and we would make her room ready. She was grateful.

Sharron had met a woman, DeAnna, while in cooking school and fell in love. They decided to get married. She was a professor and had three children—Randy, Misah, and Talia. As you can imagine, their house had a lot of energy. I was honored to be the minister for their wedding. My greatest desire was that he would find his way to an inner peace and happiness.

▶ *Exercise for the reader:*

There is something in you that is wanting to emerge. Passions within you are waiting to be revealed. Your energetic "voice" wants to be expressed. Let's look at all of the work you have done so far and get curious about manifesting something new. Write the answers to these questions in your journal:

1. What in your life, in this moment, is making you so uncomfortable that you know you have to change? (You don't have to know how.)
2. Write about an experience in your life in which you stood up for yourself, dared to risk, or opened to a possibility that scared you.
3. Recall an instance where your intuition or inner guidance called you to step out of your comfort zone.

These are just reminders that you have emerged into new realities on many occasions. In the next chapter, we are going to create a plan to support your voice coming into its own power.

CHAPTER 8

Finding My Voice

2011–PRESENT
- The Affordable Care Act is passed.
- US combat ends in Iraq.
- Osama bin Laden is killed by US forces.
- President Obama is reelected.
- The Boston Marathon bombing occurs.
- The Sandy Hook Elementary School shooting occurs.
- Janet Yellen heads the Federal Reserve.
- The Supreme Court honors same-sex marriage.
- Hilary Clinton is the Democratic presidential nominee.
- Donald Trump is elected.
- President Trump leaves the Iran nuclear deal.
- The Harvey Weinstein scandal occurs.
- The Me Too movement takes hold, and women march in solidarity.
- The Black Lives Matter movement emerges.

- Brett Kavanaugh is confirmed to the Supreme Court.
- A massacre occurs at a synagogue in Pittsburgh.
- The Mueller report on Trump and Russia is released.
- COVID-19 becomes a pandemic.
- George Floyd is killed, and people around the world protest.
- SpaceX launches astronauts to the International Space Station.
- Joe Biden is elected president.
- Insurrection occurs in Washington, DC.
- Donald Trump's second impeachment trial occurs.

This has been a decade of people wanting to be seen and heard. Activism in many forms has become apparent. Celebrities and everyday people became vocal. Women, youths, African Americans, Native Americans, and Hispanics took to the streets demanding justice and respect. The same energy was rising in me, and an inner call would not be denied.

The decade started off a little rocky. Dr. Roger had come into my office to let me know that he was not going to nominate me for an honorary doctorate. He felt he needed to nominate Reverend Ras because Ras was going to become the dean of Holmes Institute, the ministerial school. I loved Ras and thought he was brilliant, but I was a little stunned. I had spent years in leadership in the entire organization and felt I was being slighted. I didn't want to be seen as not wanting goodness for Ras, but I felt I deserved the nomination first.

I went to Dr. Marjorie, my mentor minister, and shared my feelings. I told her I wanted to stand up for myself and asked for help. She invited me to create a document of all my accomplishments in the organization over the years and present it to Roger. We agreed that this was just me asking for what I felt I deserved. I was not to have an attachment to Roger changing his mind.

I created the document and shared it with Roger. He told me he was aware of my gifts and contributions but was not changing his mind. He would nominate me the next year. I was disappointed but grateful I had not created the old pattern of swallowing my voice and pain.

Finding your voice does not ensure an outcome. Speaking your truth does not mean you will always be heard. Standing up for yourself isn't a guarantee that people won't resist you or your need. The value of discovering and sharing your voice is for you. There is a sense of freedom when you dare to respect and honor yourself. Some of the greatest people in history have been ridiculed, misunderstood, and even punished for standing up. Think about Mother Teresa, Martin Luther King Jr., Nelson Mandela, Maya Angelou, *and* their acts and their voices, which often changed the course of history.

My mother was challenged in the nursing home. She was convinced that people were stealing from her, and she believed she wasn't being taken care of. Neither was true. My uncle lived in Minneapolis, and he was an advocate for her. We were working together, and I was flying back and forth to make sure that she was okay. My brother, David, had come to reconciliation within himself and was beginning to connect with her, which made her happy. His Big Brother, Tom, had been with him through most of his life and invited him to make peace with Mom. She had really missed him. At one point, she had given him a box of all the cards and letters that she had written to him over the years, which had been returned or never delivered. She wanted him to know how much he was loved. It felt to me like things were getting better.

In the meantime, I was working a lot at Mile Hi Church, teaching and speaking. I was also feeling a call to bring my voice and expression forward. I wrote two more books and created two more music CDs. My students were hungry for support in meditation, so I created "Passages" nurturing healing in health, finances, relationship, and purpose. There were people around me who understood marketing and helped me create a website and social media presence. There was something in me that was calling me to emerge. I could feel that and still felt clueless about how to be fully realized. Honestly, I often felt a little lost.

Even though I was a part of a team at Mile Hi, I can see how this need within me to be fully expressed didn't land well with all the other ministers. No one was unkind to me. No one was separating from me, but I felt like my energy was too big and unorthodox for what had always lived in this community. I loved these people and I didn't want to make waves, but I also didn't want to pull my energy back. That recognition made me uncomfortable, but there wasn't a safe place to process it.

I was so uncomfortable that when a congregant began to stalk and threaten me, I tried to manage it.

I spoke about it to the ministers, and we agreed to be alert and to pray. On occasion someone would speak to her, and she would calm down. However, within a short period of time she would accelerate, and it got more intense over time. I became afraid for my safety, especially at night while leaving classes. I finally told the team that if we didn't tell the police, I would.

The officer who came to meet us was surprised we had taken so long to report this and helped us act. I couldn't blame anyone but myself. My need to be liked, to be seen as spiritual and loving, had pushed aside my intuitive knowing that this woman was dangerous. I vowed to myself that this would never happen again.

I was watching the same things happening in our country. Organizations, women, and other disenfranchised groups of people were wanting to step up, to be included and fully expressed. People wanted to be heard, acknowledged, and honored. Many were tired of hiding and being abused, and they were afraid. I wasn't exactly sure how this was mirroring for me, but I could feel that the energy that was going on in the country was also going on within me.

There really is no separation. *What we see and feel is a direct reflection of the experience of the whole.* The hard part is coming to terms with how to navigate the waters. This can feel like a lonely process, because only we can come to terms with an inner calling. We can reach out for support, but the ultimate choices are individual.

Carl and I had finally reached a level of connection and recommitment in our marriage. This felt great. My children were still going through their issues. Lee was having his own emotional challenges working through early childhood traumas, and he was getting support. I felt grateful that we got to talk about the things that were happening and that I could honor his courage. Sharron was still struggling but was becoming more communicative about his feelings and revelations. Plus, he had a very loving and supportive wife.

In April of 2011, Carl and I went to Minneapolis to see my mom for her ninety-second birthday. We invited my brother to come and eat with us. We all got together, and she was so happy. We took pictures, and my brother even invited us to his home. It was so beautiful. He'd made a ramp for her wheelchair to make entry easy. What I didn't realize in that moment was how her physical being was declining. Within a few days of my return to Denver, I got calls from the nursing home about her going downhill.

I went back to see her and spend time with my uncle. We realized that we needed to take care of some things. She wanted to be cremated. We took her to a cemetery where my uncle had purchased space. She picked a place where we could put her ashes and be close to my uncle's family. She also handed me folders of information on insurance and important documents. There was a part of me that didn't want to deal with this, but it was comforting to know there was clarity as her transition grew closer.

Isn't it amazing that there is no road map for nurturing the death of a parent? No one tells us how to respond mentally, emotionally, physically, or spiritually to the shifts. The only thing I know for sure is that love is the answer to every situation. I could only show up, be present, and be in a loving place of acceptance. I was not in control of anything.

I returned home, and in the next week, I got another call that the doctor wanted to put my mom on a drug that had serious side effects. I didn't know what to do. I went to see Dr. Roger. I shared my concern and that I didn't want to approve that medication. He said, "Let's pray that her soul does what it needs."

We did the prayer. I left feeling more at peace and went to lunch. When I walked into the restaurant, my phone rang. The woman calling said that my mom was unresponsive. I got back on a plane and went to be by her side. She was not given much time. My brother and I stayed in the room with her for three days straight until she passed away. Somehow, I don't even know how, I did facilitate her memorial. Her passing was opening some kind of portal within me that I didn't understand, but I knew it was a huge happening.

No one is really prepared for the death of a loved one. You can know it is coming. You can think you are ready. You can be clear that life is eternal and that only the flesh dies. That knowledge has nothing to do with the feelings of loss and grieving. There is no way to bypass missing someone you love. The seven stages of loss are real. There is no linear way to move through it. You simply must get as much support as possible and then navigate the stages:

- shock and denial
- pain and guilt
- anger and bargaining
- depression
- the upward turn
- reconstruction and working through
- acceptance and hope

Dealing with her death was big for me. I was so grateful that Dr. Roger told me to take some days off after I had come back, because I needed to process, cry, and deal with all the things that we had been through over the years. Carl's love and support were invaluable. Sometimes just holding me was the gift of the moment. Little did we know that within a year we would be going through the same process with his father.

After Mom died, David wanted to move to Colorado and expand our relationship. I was grateful. He lived with us for a year and a half until he fell in love and moved. That relationship didn't last, but we are still close and support one another.

I poured myself back into work. I thought what I needed was to do what I love. People loved my talks. I sang my prayers, and it took people to deep places. Many often bought the recordings. I felt so confident on stage, and it was so exciting to be able to bring all my gifts to the platform. It felt as if my acting, singing, modeling, and large-stage work was coalescing into magnificent presence in ministry. I had my own style of clothes, and my locks made an impression. My classes were full and powerful. My direct and clear approach inspired students to become grounded in the truth of their life and work. Many went on to become practitioners and even ministers.

All of that was true, but I kept coming home feeling tired. Carl kept saying, "You're more tired than usual. Maybe you should just go see your doctor."

I pushed back. "I have a checkup every year. I don't really need to do that."

He would get quiet but kept nudging me. Finally, I went to see the doctor and got some tests. He sat down with me and showed me a paper. "I need you to look at these numbers. They are telling us that you are headed toward Addison's disease, which is adrenal failure. You have got to quit your job."

I was stunned. "I can't quit my job. I'm a minister. I'm doing what I love."

"Well, quit your job, or you may be quitting your life," he said. I was clear that this was a big message and choice point.

I went in to talk to Dr. Roger to cut back on my workload. He was clear that I needed to take a three-month sabbatical, and this was not a request. I didn't want to take a sabbatical. I really didn't want to deal with my feelings or the emotions flooding my being. During that time off, I had to be with myself, face my fears and doubts, and open myself to clarity.

I had huge revelations. The women in my family in every generation had died overweight, ill, depressed, and emotionally unstable. I was way overweight. I was not unstable, but I was anxious. I had spent my entire life trying to prove that I was enough, trying to create my identity by being what others needed me to be.

I had been trying to have people see me, understand me, love me, and honor me by what I accomplished. I would volunteer to do more just to be acknowledged. I would try to please until my body would break down. I started seeing the patterns of how it had broken down many times because I was not listening to the universe telling me to slow down. I was exhausted because I wasn't choosing me; I was choosing to put myself last.

I began writing a new book, *I Choose Me: The Art of Being a Phenomenally Successful Woman at Home and at Work*. I journaled. I invited clients and friends to write stories of their journey to self-love. I wasn't sure what I was going to do with the book, but I was clear I needed to share my story and invite other women into the conversation about putting ourselves first.

I went back to work unclear about whether I was going to stay at my job. I was grateful that I could have honest conversations with Roger about my lack of clarity. We started with me working part-time. I could teach, speak, and support the departments I managed. It didn't take long before I started revving up again and became super busy. I really didn't know how to do it differently.

In the meantime, in my meditations I was literally getting instructions to get an office. This made no sense because I already had an office. During the holidays, Mile Hi does six candlelight services. These gatherings honor Christmas and invite people into a metaphysical understanding of the season. It is a beautiful service, and people stand in line with family members to experience it. I participated in the readings wonderfully crafted by Dr. Roger and sang with the music ministry.

I loved this entire process. It was beautifully created by the amazing team: musical director Thom Lich, production director Jennifer Burnett, Kent Rautenstraus and his band, and the incredible AV group.

The interesting thing was that every time I would come off the stage from doing the service, something happened in my solar plexus—it would constrict. I was doing work with people on mind-and-body revelations, so I knew this was important. I was uncomfortable, but nothing was wrong. Nobody was doing anything to me. Every time it happened, though, I was getting more and more anxious. At the end of the sixth service, I walked off, and I heard as clear as a bell, "You are done here." I looked around, and there was no one. I thought, *Okay, Cynthia, you're losing it. You need some rest.* After our closing ritual, I went home to rejuvenate.

That message would not leave me alone. I was to leave Mile Hi, but I had no plan. I had no idea where to go. I didn't know what I was going to do. I simply prayed during the two weeks off, and the message grew stronger. When I returned to work, I went to speak to Dr. Roger and said, "I need an exit strategy."

He was surprised and asked, "Where are you going?"

"I don't know."

"Are you starting a church?"

"No, I'm not."

He was perplexed. "Are you going to another church?"

"No, I'm not."

He looked me in the eye. "Well, then what are you doing?"

"I don't know." I was clear it sounded crazy.

I could tell we were both uncomfortable. I loved this man and this community, and it made no sense to me. However, I was clear this was a spiritual directive, and I had to be obedient and trust. We worked on a plan for me to leave at the end of June. It was important to work out a way to tell the people in the community. I was very connected to the ministry and a lot of people. I had done many things there. During this planning, the burning question became . . . where do I go from here?

I was asking every day, *What's next?* I connected with a couple of people who were getting an office. They were both practitioners and spiritual counselors, and I liked them. We found an office and split the rent. I had savings and could afford it, but I had no clients. I decorated my office and sat in it praying for guidance many days. I kept feeling that this was right for me, but I had no evidence. Coaching and counseling clients were slowly coming in, but it was not enough to sustain me financially. I was becoming a little more visible on social media, but I was not savvy enough to build a business.

When you are called to higher ground, into another realm of expression, it doesn't necessarily make sense. There's no rationality to it. You are simply called to listen and be obedient to what is pulling you forward—a vision is pulling you forward. Reverend Michael Beckwith used to say, "Pain pushes until the vision pulls." What he didn't say was that you won't necessarily have a road map. *Sometimes, you are called to say yes, act, and then surrender to the universe and the power of synchronicity.*

In the meantime, I had been doing work with women in prison and with African American women. My first book, *What Will Set You Free*, was a perfect guide for them. A friend of mine told me that the Clinton Foundation was supporting organizations that were doing different kinds of work and encouraged me to work with her to apply. We got accepted to be honored by their organization to help guide us in doing this work. Miraculously, we got an attorney and became a 501(c)(3). The Extraordinary Living Foundation was born.

We did a beta test for a year and a half in the Black community. We partnered with a community church and had women apply to come into the program. We didn't have a lot of money but got some funds from different places. The program was free to the women— we didn't want barriers to healing. The women went through six months of nutritional, mental, emotional, and physical workouts to see if we could help them change their mindsets and their ways of being.

The good news is that it was a powerful program. Women changed and had powerful healing experiences. The interesting news was that changing people's mindsets that are centuries old is not so easy. Old patterns would creep back in. After a year and a half, we were almost at a burnout point, because we couldn't get the women to stay committed. When we were supporting them weekly, it was fine. When we moved them into the next phase of the program, to use the skills they had learned, old behavior would return. I felt like I was supposed to do this work, but I didn't really know what I was doing or how to expand. That was the moment it became clear that projects and relationships really are for reasons, seasons, or lifetimes. This one was for a reason and a season.

My husband was very connected to the Transformational Leadership Council, an organization founded by Jack Canfield. I went to one of the meetings with him, and the amazing Lisa Nichols was there. I knew her from different areas but mainly from the movie *The Secret* and from watching her speak. I went up to her—I don't even know why—and I said, "I would love for you to pray for me and mentor me."

"Yes, yes. What do you want?" she asked.

I told her about my leap of faith. She said, "Well, I don't have the time to mentor, but I'm going to give you a gift. I want you to come to San Diego. I have this event called the Global Leadership Program, and you can just come for the weekend to see if there's something there for you."

My whole being lit up, and I agreed to go. The event was happening in two weeks.

I walked into a room with forty entrepreneurs, all doing different kinds of wonderful work all over the world. It was amazing. They were all incredible visionaries. I felt a little intimidated and emotional throughout the entire weekend. There was so much information. I had worked in many capacities, but it was clear that I didn't know how to run a business. One of the team members said, "You can sign up for the rest of the program. Lisa gifted you this weekend, but you would have to sign up for the rest of this program to continue."

"Well, how much does it cost?" I asked.

She said, "Fifty thousand dollars." I thought I was going to faint. I had money in savings, but I had just quit my job. I didn't have many clients to support my income. To make this kind of choice felt insane.

Once again, that inner voice was telling me to do this. I called Carl, who was in Canada doing a shoot. I told him what was going on. He asked, "What does your heart say?"

"My heart tells me to do this."

"Then you should listen."

I went to Lisa Nichols in tears and said, "I'm going to sign up for this, but I'm really scared."

She smiled and said, "It's because you don't see what I see. Our job is to get you to understand who you truly are and what you can truly accomplish."

I took a deep dive and made the investment for a year. I had to learn how to be an entrepreneur. I had to learn about the ups and downs. I had GLP coaches, and we dealt with my issues around money, what it meant to be an entrepreneur, and what it meant to have management and organizational systems. I replaced team members with experts in the field of social media and marketing. I built my mailing list and invested in automation for my newsletter and products. I even started creating a process to train coaches in my emotional freedom techniques. I wanted this to be a part of my legacy. I raised my rates as a coach and redesigned my website. I worked on my speaking skills and booked engagements for fees that felt supportive. I also became a sought-after guest on podcasts.

It was exhilarating and scary at the same time. By the end of a year, I had gotten enough clients and done enough work to pay myself back and have income. I worked hard, and many times I was frustrated. The great thing is that I was doing it for me. I had built other people's kingdoms, and now I got to see how high I could go working for myself. This was a moment of awakening. I had a vision. I spoke it. I invested in it and committed to doing the work.

The concept of investing in yourself is not one most of us have learned. There are not many places that tell you that there is no magic pill for success. The dream must be fed with commitment, action, learning, and investing in the places that will take you to higher ground. *Every successful person has invested time, energy, and money into manifesting his or her vision.*

I completed *I Choose Me* and found a hybrid publisher. I booked a VIP session with Lisa and created a strategy for my book launch and tour. She was so generous in supporting my vision. We also looked at how to create a community that would be strong and have value for its members. That session with Lisa helped *I Choose Me* become an Amazon best seller and opened the door for many invitations to speak in different parts of the world. The cool part is that I was fearless in negotiating contracts, asking for the money I deserved, and saying no to invitations that were not in alignment with my values. I had come from a place of never wanting to upset anyone, being afraid to ask for payment in keeping with my worth, and being fearful of judgment. I was becoming a woman of confidence and clarity.

Let me be clear—not everyone loved it. When I

spoke up or called people into accountability, I became the enemy. People left me and my organization. People had unkind things to say about me behind my back and sometimes publicly. I was told by many of my professional friends that this is the norm when people decide to grow. Still, it was painful. Sometimes it felt like my heart was breaking as people I loved walked away. I had to consistently look at my participation in any breakdowns. I had to reconcile my love for people with keeping my integrity. It is a very narrow path.

Right around the same time, my friend Jean Hendry and I had started talking about our passion for women. She is a leadership and curriculum specialist and presence expert, among other things, and had supported me in capturing scripts for my workshops and classes. She also helped me create my coach training and design my tour wardrobe to reflect how I wanted to be seen in the world.

We started working on Women Creating Our Futures, an organization that empowers women to live their best lives. With encouragement from my GLP coach, Jean and I created our first in-person conference. In January, we invited women to come for three days and take a deep dive into creating their futures. We had powerful speakers, musicians, and workbooks to assist women in moving beyond their fears. From there we birthed Initiating Possibilities, a ten-week mastermind program, and a program for entrepreneurs, the Academy of Women Emerging (AWE).

AWE takes women through a ten-month intensive to build their business and enhance their self-love, self-care, and spiritual practice. We have expert instructors and coaches who support them. Women have made quantum leaps in their lives and their choices. We did five years of in-person conferences, and then COVID hit. We had to quickly reinvent ourselves through virtual means.

Women look at me, and they think, *You're so confident, and you're so clear, and you're so powerful.* I tell them, "Oh, this has been evolutionary. I didn't start out this way. But everything that has happened in my life—every experience, every class, every learning, every challenge, every crisis—has led me to this moment to understand that I'm here for a purpose. I'm here because I matter. I'm here because my voice matters. I'm here because I am to bring my gifts in the most powerful way I can and teach others to do the same." It has become so clear to me that my mission is to support the awakening of humanity, especially women. My journey is not over, and I am curious about how my voice will show up in the world and model for others' possibilities.

The journey of life is a mix of experience, adventure, adversity, and growth opportunities. There is no rule book on how to manifest the life you desire. We are all individuals with different ways of being and operating. The one thing I do know is that we are all necessary. We all are essential. Otherwise, what would be the point of being on the planet at this time? The important thing for you to remember is that you have a voice. Your energy, essence, gifts, talents, and ways of expressing are unique and original. There is no one else like you on this planet. You came here to be visible and to shine. You came here to make a difference in life for yourself and for others. How you decide to share your voice is not the point. The goal is to show up and bring your most powerful self to every situation, relationship, and experience . . . bring your voice. Without you being fully expressed, someone is deprived of the gifts you came to deliver. Stand up! Stand out! Live out loud! *You are a masterpiece in the making. The world is waiting for you!*

▶ *Exercise for the reader:*

Now that you have gone through this book, let's take all the exercises and create a plan on how you want to bring your voice to the world in a more powerful way. I have included the processes to support you in this creation. Please don't rush through this. It will be your road map for the next few years.

▶ CHAPTER 1:
WHAT'S YOUR DREAM?

Now that you have shared your past, I invite you to take a moment and write down, stream of consciousness, what your ideal life would look like. You don't have to know how to get there. Make it specific! What are you doing that ignites passion within you? Where would you like to live? What kind of people do you want in your life? Do you want a family? Do you want to travel? Don't hold back.

What is your dream now? How do you want to bring impact and harmony to humanity? You don't have to have clarity. This is about creating an intention. Look at what you wrote before. Does it need to change? If so, how?

► CHAPTER 2:
REMEMBERING MOMENTS

Write down a minimum of five incidents in your childhood in which you stood up for yourself or maybe even became a rebel. Some of you will have vivid memories, and for others it will take a little longer. Maybe you ran away from home, stole a cookie from the cookie jar that your family thought they hid, pushed back on a bully, refused to wear an awful outfit your mother thought was great, told your sibling to back off, or refused to go out with someone your family loved. Whatever it is, large or small, don't discount it.

Look at the last five years. How did you show up or stand up for yourself? How can you use the first exercise and this exercise to make clear decisions about how you want to be seen in this world? What are the nonnegotiable ways you will bring your voice (music, art, activism, education, writing, teaching, and so on) and visibility to the planet?

► CHAPTER 3:
HOW DID CHALLENGE CHANGE YOU?

I encourage you to take some time and write about your experience or experiences. What was a moment in your life, environment, or family that became a turning point? What was happening? Who was involved? How did you feel? What decisions did you make? Were your choices supportive or destructive? You can use *one situation* or just allow yourself to remember the times when challenge pushed you into other ways of being. How did creativity come in? Did you learn to write? Did music become a refuge? Did you paint? Did you change your look?

Look at the challenges in your life that have caused you to grow. What did you learn? How are you responding to life differently? What choices will you make going forward because of your learnings?

▶ **CHAPTER 4:**
   VISIBILITY QUOTIENT

1. Was I encouraged as a child to be creative and stand out? If not, what kind of messaging did I receive?
2. In which moments of my life did I stand out authentically? How did it feel?
3. What are you doing right now to become more visible?

Let's celebrate the moments of your current visibility. Is it an award? Is it recognition for a project? Is it being honored for service? Do people love your website? Does your child tell you how fabulous you look? Wins are often overlooked. Please include the things, large or small, that are allowing you to shine today. This is a moment to acknowledge how fabulous you are and why your presence matters.

▶ **CHAPTER 5:**
   DREAM WRITING

Write down every dream or desire you can remember ever having. They can be silly or seemingly frivolous. Just write. You might have wanted to be a doctor, police officer, dress designer, world traveler, painter, singer, parent, spouse, dancer, island dweller, or news anchor.

Once you finish writing, circle the ones that you have experienced on any level, large or small. The circled ones are the signals from the universe that you can design your life. You can look at past vision boards or journals if you have any doubts about what has occurred.

Now, let's take the initial dream or intention and create a vision for the next one, three, and five years. Look at the items circled from Chapter 5. Anything you want to add or subtract? Now, let's dream *big*. What do you want to achieve? What kind of people do you want around you? How much money do you want to make? Who are your strategic alliances? How can you use your current visibility quotient to grow your business or dream? Make this list 50 percent achievable, and make sure there are at least fifty things on the list. As you achieve them, you will begin to cross off the goals realized. Some examples would be: I want to own a successful salon, I want to work for myself, I want to be a guest on Super Soul Sunday, I want a contract for $10,000 delivered to my door, I want to be recognized as a leader, or I want to marry my soul mate.

▶ **CHAPTER 6:**
PAUSE TOOLS

Symptoms of Needing a Pause
1. You cannot seem to shut off your mind.
2. You feel confused about the choices you need to make.
3. You do not take the time to eat properly.
4. You do not take the time to exercise.
5. You feel overwhelmed in many areas of your life.
6. You do not take the time to connect with your family.
7. You do not have a *centering* practice that supports you.

Pause Tools
1. Make yourself a priority.
2. Start your day in the quiet (minimum of *five* minutes).
3. Say *no*. It's a complete sentence.
4. Create affirmations that you say daily.
5. Engage your passion points (calendar them).
6. Commit to radical self-care.
7. Be honest with yourself.
8. Ask for help.

This is the perfect time to take a *pause* and reflect. Where are you not taking care of you? Where are you giving yourself away? What steps do you need to take to become clearer and more grounded? Review the tools from Chapter 6 and create your Care Plan.

▶ **CHAPTER 7:**
ACCESSING YOUR ENERGETIC VOICE

1. What in your life, in this moment, is making you so uncomfortable that you know you must change? (You don't have to know how.)
2. Write about an experience in your life in which you stood up for yourself, dared to risk, or opened to a possibility that scared you.
3. Recall an instance where your intuition or inner guidance called you to step out of your comfort zone.

Take this moment to write a declaration of how you will share your energy and your voice from this day forward. Look at the times you showed up for yourself in the past and assess where you might need to step up currently. You are simply planting seeds in the universe to support you in being stronger in your visibility and communication. Use the writings from Chapter 7 to assist you.

Clarity Contract: This is a commitment to yourself and how you want to show up in the world. Include your passions, purpose, affirmations, and goals. Below is one of mine, created a few years ago. Use it as a sample, but create one that has your energy and frequency:

Dear Universe:

My intention, first and foremost, is to live in a truly awakened state. To live full out, fully orbed, and fully expressed. I am committed to bringing my beauty, my light, my gifts, and my voice to this planet in extraordinary ways.

I am open and receptive to the high vision of my life in every moment. I joyously release any old patterns and behaviors that do not serve my high calling. I enthusiastically embrace the "yes" of my life in every moment. I am an intuitive vessel of the divine that listens and hears, with clarity and obedience, the divine directions of my life. I am a vibrant, vital expression of the divine, and health is the out-picturing of this truth.

I am a big *spirit with a* big *destiny. I am connected to all of life, and all of life is connected to me.*

My feelings, knowing, intuition, and desires are and have always been accurate and important.

My *very existence* inspires, empowers, and uplifts the men and women in my life beyond their wildest imaginings.

I radiate *and shine the light of God wherever I am.*

I use my talents and gifts in the following ways. I am a:

- *loving wife, mother, grandmother, great-grandmother, sister, and friend*
- *beneficial presence wherever I am*
- *recognized and renowned expert in my field*
- *writer of international best-selling and award-winning books*
- *creator of inspiring and profitable CDs and digital products*
- *creator of international products that uplift the human spirit and create health and well-being*
- *television and radio presence*
- *creator, whose worth is acknowledged with high pay, of international speaking and teaching engagements that inspire the masses*

Visibility Attributes

- *revealing love in all areas and aspects of my life*
- *committing to compassionate living*
- *caring of and for humanity*
- *teaching love in the world*
- *maintaining a loving presence*
- *being fully present in every moment*
- *communicating in the media*
- *having a powerful feminine voice*
- *being a dynamic leader*
- *being a powerful catalyst for change and transformation of myself and others*

▶ ABUNDANCE STATEMENT

I, Cynthia James, am a conduit for Spirit. I am in high service to humanity and myself. Massive streams of income flow to me easily, and I manage my money with high integrity and consciousness.

- I am worthy of wealth and money. It is my divine inheritance.
- I attract and experience sufficiency.
- Money comes to me from expected and unexpected places.

I give thanks for this or something better. And so it is!

Thank you for being a part of this book. I am so excited to see how you bring your light to this world. This is the time for your voice to make an impact. You are amazing, and you are a blessing.

About the Author

Cynthia James is a transformational specialist and one of today's brightest and most beloved inspirational teachers and leaders. Whether writing, coaching, or speaking, Cynthia is committed to guiding people and audiences through a process of inquiry, introspection, and integration for the purpose of supporting them in creating deep and lasting healing in their lives. She specializes in Emotional Integration techniques and has trained coaches around the world to do this work.

Cynthia is the author of three award-winning books: *What Will Set You Free* (English and Spanish), *Revealing Your Extraordinary Essence*, and *I Choose Me: The Art of Being a Phenomenally Successful Woman at Home and at Work*, which achieved number one best-seller status in the New Age, Spiritual, and Self-Help categories. It was also a finalist in the International Book Awards. She also has a children's book, *You Are Loved*, created to support young girls in recognizing their value.

A sought-after radio guest, Cynthia has given hundreds of interviews and has cohosted both a radio talk show and a television talk show pilot in Los Angeles with Cristina Ferrare.

Ms. James has completed two master's degree programs: one in consciousness studies from the Holmes Institute, where she was awarded the Honor of Distinguished Alumni, and the other in spiritual psychology from the University of Santa Monica. She has uniquely combined the creative arts with innovative therapeutic techniques to bring powerful personal growth and expansion to individuals of all ages, cultures, and lifestyles. Her books, music, and meditation products have supported individuals and groups around the world.

An ordained licensed minister, Cynthia is a frequent presenter and workshop facilitator at New Thought churches around the world. She is a featured presenter with the Shift Network and Humanity's Team summits, two of the largest and most successful providers of virtual courses, online workshops, and teleseminar events taught by experts in the areas of spirituality and personal growth. She also leads pilgrimages to sacred sites around the world.

She has facilitated hundreds of workshops, seminars, and keynote addresses at popular venues such as Celebrate Your Life, the Omega Institute, and the Gift in Shift. She has conducted workshops and staff retreats for the Colorado Behavioral Healthcare Council, Women's Success Forum, School of Mines, and the Children's Hospital. Cynthia made her living as a successful actress for many years and was a cohost on a television pilot for Disney in Los Angeles. She has appeared in the films *Sacred Journey of the Heart* and *Leap! A Quantum Awakening.*

Cynthia has been a speaker and presenter and consistent guest of the esteemed Transformational Leadership Council, a by-invitation-only group of authors, speakers, coaches, trainers, researchers, consultants, and other leaders in the fields of personal and professional development, which was established by Jack Canfield in July of 2004. She is an accomplished singer and songwriter having traveled all over the world.

Along with her husband, Carl Studna, she cofacilitates powerful relationship-building and leadership-development courses, both online and in person.

Author photo © Carl Studna Photographer